D1572175

The Social License

The Social License

How to Keep Your Organization Legitimate

John Morrison

First published 2014 by
PALGRAVE MACMILLAN

Palgrave Macmillan in the UK is an imprint of Macmillan Publishers Limited, registered in England, company number 785998, of Houndmills, Basingstoke, Hampshire RG21 6XS.

Palgrave Macmillan in the US is a division of St Martin's Press LLC, 175 Fifth Avenue, New York, NY 10010.

Palgrave Macmillan is the global academic imprint of the above companies and has companies and representatives throughout the world.

Palgrave® and Macmillan® are registered trademarks in the United States, the United Kingdom, Europe and other countries

ISBN 978–1–137–37071–6

This book is printed on paper suitable for recycling and made from fully managed and sustained forest sources. Logging, pulping and manufacturing processes are expected to conform to the environmental regulations of the country of origin.

A catalogue record for this book is available from the British Library.

A catalog record for this book is available from the Library of Congress.

Typeset by MPS Limited, Chennai, India.

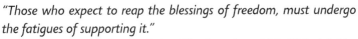

"Those who expect to reap the blessings of freedom, must undergo the fatigues of supporting it."

Thomas Paine, *The American Crisis*, Philadelphia,
12 September 1777

For Fiona and our children (Caitlin, Roisin, Felix, and Theo)

Contents

Acknowledgments

There are many I wish to thank for their support. As icons, I would like to honor the bravery of different peoples, such as those of the Niger Delta (and in particular Ken Saro-Wiwa) and the people of Bhopal in India, whose suffering helped shape the consciousness behind what we might now call the global business and human rights movement.

At a personal level I owe a lot to Anita and Gordon Roddick, Geoffrey Chandler, Mary Robinson, and John Ruggie for their leadership; and to countless others with whom I work.

In relation to this book, there are many I would like to thank, including: Motoko Aizawa, Chris Anderson, Leeora Black, Phil Bloomer, Richard Boele, Lucy Chandler, Aidan Davy, Kathryn Dovey, Bjorn Edlund, Peter Frankental, Bennett Freeman, Doran Hanlon, Mark Hodge, Frances House, Scott Jerbi, Chris Jochnick, Nick Killick, Justine Lacey, Amy Lehr, Rae Lindsay, Chris Marsden, Leslie Morrison, Simon Morrison, Tamsine O'Riordan, Malin Oud, Gerald Pachoud, Ed Potter, Lucy Purdon, John Ruggie, Kelly Davina Scott, Haley St. Dennis, Elizabeth Stone, Salil Tripathi, Margaret Wachenfeld, Toby Webb, and Claire White.

Michael Addo, David Angell, Sean Ansett, Turid Arnegaard, Cindy Berman, Adam Cramer, Elizabeth Dahlin, Tom Dodd, Michel Doucin, Janneke Faber, Liesel Filgueiras, Remy Friedmann, Christian Frutiger, Juan Gonzalez Va lero, Adam Greene, Alexandra Guaqueta, Paul Hohnen, Marie-France Houde, Isobelle Jacques, Bengt Johansson, Heather Johnson, Margaret Jungk, Dwight Justice, Christine Kaufmann, Georg Kell, Catharina Kipp, Madeleine Koalick, Khalid Koser, Ramanie Kunanayagam, Ken Larson, Markus Loening, Jens Munch Lund-Nielsen, Tam Nguyen, Bonnie Nixon,

Are-Jostein Norheim, Julia Purcell, Gwendolyn Remmert, Angela Rivas, Simone Rocha Pinto, Nils Rosemann, Hege Rottingen, Robert San Pe, Elin Schmidt, Puvan Selvanathan, Charlotta Spolander, Susan Stormer, Pavel Sulyandziga, Lisa Svensson, Claire Wallace-Jones, Dewi-vande Weerd, Rajiv Williams, Brent Wilton, Charlotte Wolf, Yann Wyss.

Beyond this, there are many others who have guided me over the last 20 years in many different ways (and who cannot be blamed in any way for this book), including: Kate Allen, Philip Alston, Per Uno Alm, Lucy Amis, Robert Archer, David Arkless, Chris Avery, Graham Baxter, Philippa Birtwell, Christine Bader, Jim Baker, Lakshmi Bhatia, Vanessa Bissessur, Tom Blumenau, Frans Bouwen, Vicky Bowman, Zrinka Bralo, Peter Brew, Pins Brown, Simon Burall, Doug Cahn, Lynn Carter, Kavita Chetty McRorie, Leila Choukroune, Abrar Chowdhury, Andrew Clapham, Bob Corcoran, Rachel Davis, Aidan Davy, Sumi Dhanarajan, Luis Fernando de Angulo, Kaj Embren, Ravi Fernando, Teresa Fogelberg, Ian Gearing, Elodie Grant Goodey, Lois Graessle, Donna Guest, Mei Li Han, James Hathaway, Isabel Hilton, Paul Hohnen, Christian Honore, Sam Hoskins, Nick Howen, Christine Jesseman, Alan Lerberg Jorgensen, Neil Kearney, Deanna Kemp, Tom Kennedy, Irene Khan, Nick Killick, Wambui Kimathi, Rose Kimotho, Morten Kjaerum, Jody Kollapen, David Laws, Sheldon Leader, Klaus Leisinger, Gareth Llewellyn, Rebecca MacKinnon, Marcela Manubens, Peter MacDonald, Steve McIvor, Aidan McQuade, Bonita Meyersfeld, Amol Mehra, Viraf Mehta, Anton Mifsud-Bonnici, Alan Miller, Felix Morka, Susan Morgan, Dorje Mundle, Javier Mujica, Stuart Murray, Michael Nolte, Ron Nielsen, Roel Nieuwenkamp, Anders Nordstrom, Mark Nordstrom, Steve Ouma, Chip Pitts, Ron Popper, Michael Posner, Kavita Prakesh-Mani, D.J. Ravandran, Usha Ramanathan, Anita Ramasastry, Yuri Ramkissoon, Soraya Ramoul, Caroline Rees, Joanna Reyes, Kenneth Roth, Philip Rudge, Jill Rutter, Lyndall Sachs, Jon Samuel, David Schilling, Matthew Shreader, Kelly Davina Scott, Nick Scott-Flynn, Andrea Shemberg, John Sherman, Smita Singh, Sune Skadegaard Thorsen, Annette Stube, Daniel Taillant, Mark Taylor, Ruth Valentine, Auret Van Heerden, Andrew Vickers, Claude Voillat, Wilma Wallace, Margot Wallstrom, Yasmin Waljee, Halina Ward, Lene Wendland, Elaine Weidman, Neill Wilkins, Luke Wilde, Peter Woicke, Katryn Wright, Hnin Wut Yee, Ursula Wynhoven, Melike Yetken, and Vanessa Zimmerman. There are others, some I cannot name.

Finally to acknowledge all the support of friends and family and those who spend weekends with us in Sussex, UK. Eating, camping, running on the Downs and even fishing expeditions are valuable sources of fun. Those who visit Lewes in Sussex will see that Thomas Paine appears on the town's own unofficial currency as well as being the name of a beer from the local Harveys brewery (Paine lived in Sussex between 1768 and 1774, during which time he wrote his first political work). For anyone wishing to apportion original blame for this book, they can probably start with too many years in local pubs drinking that beer.

Preface

I have spent the past 25 years working in the field of human rights, initially in refugee resettlement but for nearly 15 years on the issue of business responsibilities towards human rights from the vantage point of civil society, international organizations, governments, and business itself. This book is highly personal and subjective: it draws on my own experience as well as concepts and examples that have inspired me in trying to consider the societal impacts of different types of organizations.

I have seen occasions where business itself has stepped up voluntarily to show real leadership when government officials, elected or not, have demurred from doing so. Alternatively, I have seen times when business has lobbied hard against changes that have been needed to advance wider societal interests. Similarly, non-governmental organizations (NGOs) play an essential role in holding both governments and business to account, but NGOs themselves can also be highly unaccountable and they do not always represent the interests of the most vulnerable.

The book takes the broad concept of "social license" as a way of considering how different activities may acquire or lose legitimacy in the eyes of society. Whilst the term "social license" is a relatively new one, I link it to a much older idea—that of the "social contract" that binds society itself and also legitimizes the role of what I consider to be one of the most fundamental of all organizations, that of government. I believe that thinking about social license in relation to the social contract raises some interesting ideas and questions for all types of organizations in how their activities might be sustainable in social terms.

The social license relates to the activities of any organization. Obtaining and securing the social license cannot be directly managed or self-awarded; rather, it is the result of interactions between a number of factors that will be explored in greater depth in this book. It is these factors that organizations can manage, not the social license itself. The fact is that it is much easier to notice the absence of the social license than to recognize its presence. The presence of the social license might be described as an equitable balance, or harmony, between different societal interests that allows a specific activity to continue and to thrive. However, as the social license is dynamic, it can always be withdrawn by society.

I have long felt the gap in our understanding of how the world operates from debates about business and society in particular. The concept of corporate social responsibility has taken us only so far while emerging work on business and human rights has taken us much further, in my opinion. Perhaps some of the ideas in this book represent my own reflections on the still wider question— what does it mean for the activities of any organization to be legitimate in societal terms and what can organizational managers and decision-makers do about it? What follows are not the reflections of an academic, nor is this book meant to be a management guide. Rather, the story I tell is aimed at shifting our collective thinking and to start asking some of what I see as the right questions.

Some of the ideas I present throughout the book are inspired by my current role as Executive Director of the Institute for Human Rights and Business. However, the views expressed here are wholly my own as are the mistakes I have made. I am very interested in any feedback and views these ideas stimulate—these can be tweeted to me at @jomo1966.

Part **1**

Introduction

Macondo

"Their Power in the utmost Bounds of it, is limited to the Publick good of Society"[1]

John Locke (1689)

20 April 2010

At 8.50 pm the rig personnel felt "a kick." They had been monitoring the cement pumped down to the bottom of the production casing of Block 252 of the Mississippi Canyon in the Gulf of Mexico, one of the deepest deepwater oil wells in the world. The rig was 48 miles off shore, in 4,992 feet of water and drilling to a depth of 20,600 feet.[2] The jolt they felt was an imbalance between the pressure of the drilling fluid and the hydrocarbons in the reservoir at the bottom of the well deep below the sea. Within ten minutes these hydrocarbons had flowed up the riser onto the rig floor and caused the rig to explode—a chain of events that would kill 11 platform workers and cause the largest offshore oil spill in US history. The platform was the *Deepwater Horizon*, contracted by BP to exploit the "Macondo Prospect" (named after Gabriel García Márquez's fictional Colombian village). The rest is a matter of recent history.

The next few months would be bad for the company. Few US stakeholders would be prepared to defend the company's safety record (largely due to the Texas City and Prudhoe Bay disasters which had preceded that in the

Gulf of Mexico[3]) and even worse, BP's four main competitors were willing to go to Congress to testify against the company for not meeting industry standards.[4] BP faced between $20 and $37 billion in total liabilities—a large sum even for an oil company.[5] The story is now well known. The then CEO, Tony Hayward, stumbled when trying to explain the accident and BP's response to the wider world.[6] By this time, it had become a media feeding frenzy—his tone was perceived to be aloof and there was virtually no one anywhere in the world who was willing to stand in front of a camera and defend his company, other than those his company paid to do so (i.e. his employees and lawyers). Within weeks, a new CEO was in place.

What lessons can be drawn from this example? First, that the risk to human life was not perceived to have been managed well enough by a company that had gone through a cycle of aggressive acquisitions and then cost-cutting. This is not to suggest that BP intended any adverse outcome to occur. Few companies are cynical enough to have such a goal. But the outcome was not anticipated, or if it was, the probability, the company thought, was negligible. Second, so whilst BP's problems all had a technical element at source, they were undoubtedly compounded and magnified by something greater—the social, political, and legal context of the USA. In other words, whilst the problem was technical, the management implications of such a technical risk had a direct bearing on the expectations that society had and still has on the company.

It is important to remember that in 1984 Union Carbide, whose health and safety breaches in Bhopal, India, caused the death of over 3,000 people, arguably faced much less of a reputational issue in the US market than did BP. The Bhopal disaster was a generation earlier and on a different continent but whilst it has left a strong legacy of societal expectation in India, the actions of a US company abroad have left fewer expectations in the home country. So public and political sentiment can be fickle and highly domestic in focus. Legal regimes differ considerably around the world, and therefore so does non-technical risk. However, a human life is a human life and recent efforts between governments, within the United Nations and elsewhere, make the lessons of the Gulf of Mexico increasingly relevant to anyone anywhere in the world.[7] Both these cases, BP and Union Carbide, illustrate how legitimacy in the eyes of society can be a material issue for a business. It can cost the company not just in terms of immediate financial damages but also in terms of its future operations. For example, a recent study has estimated that conflicts with local communities can cost mining companies up to US $20 million per week when large projects are delayed. Legitimacy and community relations can have real commercial value.[8]

And so to the focus of this book: the "social license." In recent years the concept of the "social license to operate" has arisen within the mining sector in particular. The concept has been defined in various ways, as will be discussed in the next chapter, but has broadly meant "the extent to which a corporation is constrained to meet societal expectations and avoid activities that societies (or influential elements within them) deem unacceptable."[9] This book endeavors to take the social license concept much wider and deeper, showing its relevance not just to all business sectors but also to the activities of governments, civil society organizations, trade unions, faith groups, communities, and other actors. My own experience of working in and with all of these types of organizations suggests to me that a good deal of their legitimacy, in the eyes of society at least, arises from their social license. As I will discuss, the concept is perhaps much less woolly and intangible than some might appreciate if it is pinned to older philosophical ideas—in particular the idea of the social contract between individuals in society.

When taking over from John Browne as CEO of BP in 2007, Tony Hayward made the comment that BP had "too many people trying to save the world."[10] My contention is the opposite. In fact BP would have benefitted from having more people who really understood social risk and social impact in a global sense, and the company would come to suffer as a consequence. Ironically, a few years earlier, BP had had more of these socially minded people, but many left as part of the "de-Browneification" of the company when Sir John Browne stood down as CEO (for unrelated reasons), according to some observers.[11] As I will argue, being part of global solutions and not global problems is much more than an issue of "public relations," "corporate social responsibility," or "spin," but about legitimacy that can be earned through knowledge and actions, not clever advertising or aggressive lawyers.

"World savers" and "tree huggers" are two of the many derogatory terms that some who think they have "hard skills" (e.g. geologists, engineers, bankers, lawyers) throw at those with "softer skills" (e.g. anthropologists, sociologists, political scientists, NGO types). However, there is much in the world today to suggest that human skills (a better term than "soft skills"), or more particularly knowledge and ability about how to generate and maintain legitimacy in eyes of fellow humans, will be skills that both businesses and governments will crave and value in years to come at least as much as they value clever geologists. There were ample opportunities to demonstrate the lack of such skills during the summer of 2010.

There are a number of associated questions that I will return to:

- How much knowledge should an organization have of its social risks and impacts?
- In particular, what priority should be given to risks that might have a significant impact on human life or wellbeing?
- How does an organization know that its measures to mitigate such risks are adequate in the eyes of others?
- How transparent should it be about its knowledge of these risks and associated mitigation measures? How should such disclosures be made?
- How should others outside the organization be involved in this whole process of identifying and managing risk on an ongoing basis? What responsibility are these stakeholders given and what legitimacy might be conferred on the organization as a result?

And so a final word on BP. It is a company with many technically competent people who often get it right. But it has had its share of problems. It pays its taxes, it is accountable to its shareholders and to the home and host governments under which it operates. It is no longer saddled with issues of colonial legacy in different parts of the world. There have been periods in its relatively recent history when BP has shown progressive good sense—often at the local level. The company carried out what may have been the world's first human rights impact assessment was carried out in Tangguh in West Papua, Indonesia, during the late 1990s as well as the legal assurances made to Amnesty International in relation to the Baku–Tbilisi–Ceyhan pipeline (between the Caspian Sea and the Mediterranean).[12] Similarly, BP has been one of the most active companies in leading the development of the Voluntary Principles on Security and Human Rights in countries such as Colombia.[13]

The whole industry, and not just BP, has some fundamental choices to make. They have traditionally seen such issues as *Deepwater Horizon* in primarily health and safety terms—which of course it is at its core. Health and safety puts the protection of an individual above all other considerations (or at least it should) and is based on a methodology of prevention and due diligence to minimize risk and take associated mitigations. But of course major social impacts can be more than health and safety—for local communities they can be as diverse as impacts on water, land, livelihoods, freedom of expression, or personal security. Many businesses currently see these wider relationships with society largely as an issue of public relations (PR) or public affairs. PR traditionally puts the interests of the organization above all other considerations: they are the "client" are they not? Health and safety is "human centric," whilst PR is most certainly not. If this book is to achieve anything, it is to get organizations to think about all their social relationships with the same seriousness that they already approach health and safety. You don't have to kill or injure your own workers to have a social impact, and therefore prevention and due diligence need to underpin all social relationships.

In 2010 there was no externally acknowledged process to bring the different perspectives on the social risks of deepwater drilling before the Gulf of Mexico disaster. In fact, there is still little such activity in most countries even if there is now more debate in the USA. Nor are there many processes that bring the competing companies together with other "stakeholders" impartially to discuss other high-risk activities associated with the oil industry, such as fracking and coal-bed methane, tar sands, arctic or oil exploration in rural, environmentally challenging contexts (such as East Africa). However, such processes can exist—often when governments exert a little pressure. Such "multi-stakeholder" processes do exist on two very material issues for the sector: revenue transparency[14] and the issue of public and private security forces.[15] It is less conceivable that BP's competitors could have come to the US Congress and criticized the company for being "below industry standards" on the issues of security or revenue transparency. Two prominent examples I have in mind here are the Voluntary Principles on Security and Human Rights, and the Extractive Industries Transparency Initiative. So, why then do oil companies not move to create such consensus mechanisms for other high-risk issues—such as deepwater drilling?

The answer to this question is both very complex (there are of course a range of technical and competitive issues) and strikingly simple. Business has not come together with other stakeholders to trade some of their individual power for a pooling of some non-technical risk because the process of doing so is very new, is not valued or understood by enough CEOs, and requires a vast range of "human skills." Businesses will come together when governments make them do so, or the public outcry is so vehement, as in the case of the aftermath of the Bangladesh clothing factory collapse in May 2013 in which over 1,100 people died.[16] Most businesses will not surrender even a little of their power for strategic reasons alone, although the time is coming when they might in order to increase the likelihood that their activities might enjoy greater social license.

Governments too, within the context of civil uprisings across North Africa, the Middle East, Turkey, and Brazil, cannot rely on a four- or five-year trip to the ballot box alone as sufficient social legitimacy:

> It is not enough that leaders submit themselves for periodical elections. Democracy demands a commitment to pluralism, the submission of the powerful as well as the weak to the rule of law, protections for minorities and respect for cultural and ethnic difference.[17]

Most modern ideas of what government and democracy are rest upon the idea that governments govern through the consent of the people. Through history, rulers have claimed divine right or historical precedent to maintain their hegemony. Expectations in virtually every country and culture have changed: some form of consent is both the visceral and intellectual, if not the legal, and constitutional, norm. Building on the work of thinkers such as Thomas Hobbes, John Locke, and Jean-Jacques Rousseau, any government can be seen as a manifestation of a social contract between individuals within a society.

Governments might be all-powerful and autocratic (as Hobbes believed), or a much more consensual republic (as Rousseau envisaged). Similar thinking also comes from Asia. Confucius wrote much about governance, with ideas similar to many Western thinkers on the need for wise mandarins ruling for the greater good of society. The social contract was akin to the thinking behind Hobbes' *Leviathan*: the wise men govern (and it was men), the people obey and in return the rice bowl remains full in Confucian terms. In India, Gandhi had his own idea of trusteeship that took yet another slant on the social contract, different from that of China and the West. For Gandhi, trusteeship was a society in which owners of capital had a moral duty to safeguard the interests of the less fortunate, and they needed to operate as if the assets under their command were held in trust.[18]

What is true of all ideas of social contract is that there is an unwritten contract between the governed, upon which the legitimacy of the government rests—whether this be to guard against the selfishness of individuals (Hobbes) or to ensure that the rice bowl remains full (Confucius) or that the wealthy will take care of the whole of society (Gandhi). Implicit, of course, in all these approaches, is that the unwritten contract can, in extreme circumstances, be revoked by the people, whether through elections, peaceful protests, or revolution. Perhaps then we can also start to understand social license in such terms, as a reflection of a strong social contract, but also as a license that can be revoked if the pre-existing social contract is not adequately respected or is itself rotten.

This then is the basis for my book. Over recent years the concept of "social license" has arisen to describe the legitimacy of certain activities in social terms. For any organization—a company, a government agency, or an NGO—wishing to enjoy a social license for a specific activity, it needs to manage key aspects of its relationship with groups in society. Perhaps most fundamental, as will be set out in this book, are those impacted by the activity itself, those we might call the "affected rights-holders." I believe these relationships are modern forms of social contract thinking, although the nature of each relationship with the contract will be different for governments, businesses, and NGOs. This book aims to help any of these organizations wishing to better understand and manage their social relationships and to ask questions, the responses to which are most likely to engender strong social license.

2

The social license

"Nemo judex in causa sua"

(No one can be judge of their own cause)

In his statement to the court in 1995, shortly before his execution, Ken Saro-Wiwa stated:

> I predict that the scene here will be played and replayed by generations yet unborn. Some have already cast themselves in the role of villains, some are tragic victims, some still have a chance to redeem themselves. The choice is for each individual.[1]

In this extract from his final words, Ken Saro-Wiwa captures something of his legacy—a community's struggle for environmental and social justice but also one in which powerful actors have real choices. In his final statement, Ken blamed the Shell Oil Company for what was wrong with the country—the environmental degradation, the corruption, the oppression—but, fundamentally, he was blaming the unaccountable Nigerian state. The Nigerian government had betrayed the social contract that had created it, was no longer the servant of the Nigerian people but had become its oppressor. Shell was seen to be heavily complicit with that arrangement. The role played by Shell executives during 1994 and 1995 has been the subject of legal cases, out-of-court settlements, and so on, but what is clear—in my opinion at least—is that the company lost the social license for its activities in that part of the Niger Delta because it was perceived to be so close to what was then an unaccountable Nigerian state. Even today the joint venture between the Nigerian state and Shell has been unable to drill for oil in Ogoniland or even adequately repair pipelines that pass through it. Instead the region has remained unsettled for much of the past 20 years, beset by the bunkering of oil, criminal gangs, and a much more complex and tangled mess of relationships.[2] This demonstrates that once a social license has been lost it can be very hard to regain, even with the best of practices, and now with a democratically elected Nigerian state.

When I started working as the human rights campaigner for The Body Shop International plc in the late 1990s (a unique title in a company to be sure, even nowadays), there were many things that were unusual about the role. First, London-listed multinational companies (with shops in over 50 markets worldwide) did not usually have human rights campaigners. Second, the owners of the company—Anita and Gordon Roddick—were as inspired by social justice as they were by making a profit; in fact they saw no contradiction between the two. This balance between the financial, social and environmental performance of the company was reflected in the products, staff training, and communicating with customers.

To sit in The Body Shop and pen letters for the Roddicks to send to Sir Mark Moody-Stuart at Shell about ongoing concerns in the Niger Delta was a novel experience—one multinational company writing to another on issues of human rights many years before most companies had even engaged on the issue. Years later, I met the former Shell Head of Public Affairs and we reflected that we had in effect been writing to each other during the late 1990s. The link between The Body Shop and Ken Saro-Wiwa and his Ogoni people was a real one. The Roddicks had been made honorary Ogoni Chiefs, and it was my predecessor Richard Boele, whose Body Shop mobile phone had rung to inform Ken Wiwa junior that his father had been executed when they were both at the Commonwealth Heads of State meeting in New Zealand trying to shame the international community enough to intervene.

To this day, a social license for oil exploration still does not exist for oil production in Ogoniland. Writing in 2011, the United Nations commented on some of the roots of the widespread pollution and how standards in the oil industry have changed through time. What used to be acceptable behavior by business 30 years ago is no longer the case now. Today, social license is a concept cited by oil companies even if its full meaning has yet to emerge.[3]

What is the "social license to operate"?

When it comes to the operations of companies, it is much easier to see where the social license has been lost than to point to examples where it is still present in operational terms. Before I go further, it should be underlined that the loss of social license is as much an issue in Europe or North America as it is in the Global South. Many times the social license is in place and therefore invisible in most respects. But a well-documented example of loss of social license was the loss of public confidence for genetically modified crops in Europe, even though there was little or no evidence of possible harm. In the UK, this can be contrasted with greater public confidence in other areas of science—such as in vitro fertilization (IVF) and embryology—where more effort has been made to inform the public of the risks and benefits.[4]

What are the new structures through which organizations will develop and mediate their "social license" for activities on an ongoing basis? Although I focus mainly on the social license of non-state actors, and in particular business, the concept is also valid for state actors, and so some examples are given to highlight what this might mean. What social license does not mean, for any actor, is a diminution of existing legal and political duties and responsibilities. In fact, I will argue that a deeper and more correct understanding of social license—as a modern manifestation of the social contract—is likely to clarify existing and future legal obligations rather than undermine them.

This book is not about the "social license to operate" specifically, as this is a term largely invented by business, for business. However, I need first to explain the inspiration that the "to operate" concept has given me, before expanding on a wider definition of the "social license."

The term "social license to operate" seems to have arisen in its current form from the mining industry, and, in particular, in relation to operations in Australia and Canada since the 1990s, although some also relate it to the oil industry in the same period.[5] One of the first, if not the first, explicit uses of the term is credited to Jim Cooney, an international mining executive, who used the term in a meeting with the World Bank in 1997.[6]

Two of the early exponents of the social license to operate in the mining sector have been Robert Boutilier and Ian Thomson with their work in Australia, Bolivia, and Mexico over a 15-year period.[7] Their work has focused on four factors for mining operations: economic legitimacy, socio-political legitimacy, interactional trust, and institutionalized trust. Leeora Black, a leading academic observer of the phenomenon, defines the social license to operate as "the negotiation of equitable benefits and impacts of a company in relation to its stakeholders, over the near and longer term." It is essentially a political idea, "if all politics is about the distribution of benefits and impacts, then the social license is inherently political."[8] She notes that a social license to operate can range from informal, like an implicit social contract, to formal, like a community benefit agreement.

When defining the concept for a business audience, Black stresses the following:

> The social license to operate is not a piece of paper or a document like a government license. It's a form of social acceptance or approval that companies or projects earn through consistent and trustworthy behaviour and interactions with their stakeholders. It's a socially constructed perception that your company or project has a legitimate place in that community.[9]

Use of the social license to operate concept

Leeora Black is amongst those giving the specific "social license to operate" concept substance over recent years as it relates to the mining sector. Although this has mainly been for a business audience, she has not demurred from investing it with political and substantive content. She stresses:

- Social license is not a synonym for acts of philanthropy or community investment;
- Addressing power imbalances is a key component and sometimes requires powerful actors, such as business, to cede power to communities;
- Stakeholders and communities are self-defining, they cannot be defined by a business.

Bruce Harvey, a long-time Australian mining hand, puts the traditional business perspective on social license to operate very nicely and also brings in its relationship to legal license:

> If we think about what's happened in the world in the last 50 years, previously the resource sector secured its license to operate at the discretion of government. In fact, we still do. And that's called a legal license and permits and licenses are granted and we live up to the expectations and they are maintained. But in the world of globalization and in an increasing world of scrutiny and mobilization of local voices, if you don't have the broad based support of local people for what you want to do, then you won't get your legal license.[10]

During the early part of the 21st century the term social license to operate has been used more generally by a range of actors often, but not always, with a focus on the extractive sectors (oil, gas, and mining). While the term gets referenced increasingly outside of the extractive sectors, it does not necessarily mean the same thing to everyone, nor do they necessarily agree with various industry definitions. The first use by the Organisation for Economic Co-operation and Development (OECD) seems to be in 2002,[11] and more recently the United Nations Special Representative on Business and Human Rights, Professor John Ruggie, used the term several times during his own mandate (2005–11).[12] It has also been observed by other important United Nations experts such as James Anaya, the Special Rapporteur on the Rights of Indigenous Peoples.[13]

The concept has occasionally been used more generally, well beyond the extractive sectors. For example, when discussing agriculture, the social license to operate has been defined in very broad terms as: "a shorthand way to describe the latitude that society allows its citizens to exploit resources for their private purposes."[14] Such a broad and unspecific definition is, in my view, unhelpful and also risks undermining other fundamental licenses—in particular the legal license founded in local and international law. So, for any ongoing use of the term, and particularly if it is to be extended into new arenas (as it is in this book), then a clearer definition is essential.

Critiques of the "social license to operate" concept

There have a number of criticisms of the "social license to operate" concept. A paper published by the international NGO Oxfam in 2011 describes it in the following way:

Whilst there is no standard or generally accepted definition for "social license [to operate]," it is commonly viewed as existing when a development project has the on-going acceptance of a project by local communities. Social license to operate is in addition to the governmental or legally granted right to operate. Although social license suggests a positive relationship between a company and its neighbours, corporations when pressed are rarely willing to equate social license with community consent—that is, corporations aren't willing to withdraw operations in places where communities are opposed to their presence.[15]

It is for similar reasons that I include consent as a core definitional component of my own definition of the social license which I will be developing for this book and I agree that it is absent in most existing definitions. If we consider social license in a wider range of contexts, and not just communities and extractive projects, the importance of consent can be illustrated too—for example, consumer data privacy and the internet, or medical information in relation to pharmaceutical trials. However, although the absence of consent is equivalent to a veto in some contexts, it is not in others. So whilst consent is intrinsic to any comprehensive understanding of social license, it needs to be well understood as it might be legitimate for governments, businesses, or others to proceed without local social license or local consent in some contexts.

Some have criticized social license to operate from a business perspective. For example:

> This is a way for opponents of certain industries or projects to de-legitimise a business by going around and proclaiming that its social license [to operate] has been or should be withdrawn. And although the term sounds technical and legitimate, it is calling for a withdrawal of something that does not exist by those who were powerless to give it. Although this notion is clearly becoming fashionable, and some business leaders may see some PR advantages to it, they should resist its superficial appeal.[16]

This quote brings in the concept of legitimacy, which—I agree—is also core to any understanding of the social license. It also points, rightly, to the poorly defined nature of the social license to operate concept, but it fails when it understands power only in its traditional sense of legal license:

> After all, New Zealand already has a "social license to operate" and it is made up of laws passed by Parliament, consisting of elected representatives

and the courts that enforce them. For anyone caring about the rule of law, the social license is a concept that should be viewed with suspicion.[17]

This is a narrow definition of the social license to operate as purely a legal license. Legal license is itself complex as companies have responsibilities not only in terms of local laws but also in terms of international law, such as human rights. To limit a company's responsibility to "following local law" is to turn back discussions of corporate responsibility 20 years (to the time of Ken Saro-Wiwa's untimely death) and does little to help any international company with its key social dilemmas, even those operating in New Zealand. If following local law was all it took, many of the current dilemmas faced by communities and businesses alike would not exist.

There is not yet a large body of literature on social license to operate, since the term is a relatively new one. However, the two criticisms quoted above are representative of wider critiques that exist and are illuminating when considered together. The first, from the NGO perspective, sets up an opposition between social license to operate and consent. The second, from a business perspective, sets up an opposition between social license to operate and legal license. Both of these oppositions, I argue, are fallacious if we take a more substantive approach to social license in the way I think it should be defined. As already stated, social license and consent should be very much aligned. In fact, consent should be a precondition for any claim as to the existence of social license (in particular local consent). In relation to the second claim, a broader understanding of the social license does not undermine or confuse pre-existing duties for companies as part of their legal license, but—as I will seek to show—the legal license itself has its own inherent contradictions. These spill over into social license when we think of international legal norms which have yet to become binding criminal, civil, or administrative law. The two critiques contradict each other to some extent, as consent itself is often a legal requirement.

"social license and consent should be very much aligned"

A definition of "social license"

In this book I take the narrower concept of "social license to operate" and seek to move it beyond the oil, gas, and mining sectors where it has been most commonly referenced to all other business sectors and beyond, to other types of organization. Therefore, whilst many of the examples given come from business, it is also argued that all organizations need to consider the parameters of their "social license." The words "to operate" are deliberately dropped, as I see the concept as having a wider utility than specific operations, although the term needs to relate to some specific activity or another. In other words, social license relates to what an organization *does* and not to what it *is*. Nor do I concur with all aspects of the way the social license to operate concept has been used in its business-only existence to date. Some of the associated concepts to be considered, such as legitimacy, relate to the governance and purpose of the organization itself, but for social license to be meaningful as a concept it has to relate to a specific activity: a specific project, policy, law, product, initiative, operation, campaign, or whatever.

Whilst I agree that the narrower concept of social license has related to specific social groups, my own broader concept does not limit this to local community groups. Other social groups (or their proxies) can be mediators of social license, such as NGOs, interest groups, trade unions, religious groups, media, and the wider public. Some of these social groups might be described as "stakeholders"—groups (often represented by organizations) affected by or having some engagement in the activity, a subset of whom will be "rights-holders"—individuals, workers, or communities with human rights (not the organizations that represent them).

Implicit in this, of course, is the fact that not all social groups will align or be in agreement with each other on issues of social license. Even under definitions of social license to operate in the mining sector and related impacts on specific local communities, these communities might well be engaging with international NGOs, investors, and so on.

So, I define the social license as describing the sum of expectations between an organization and relevant social groups (usually represented by other organizations) in relation to a specific activity or set of related activities. Preconditions for the social license to exist are:

- All the organizations—both those involved in the activity and those representing the social groups affected—perceive both each other and the activity itself to have sufficient *legitimacy* to proceed;
- There is sufficient *trust* between all the relevant organizations;
- The organizations representing the affected social groups have *consented* to the activity in question.

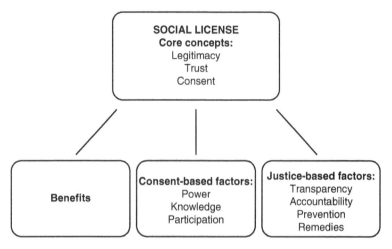

FIG 2.1 / Concepts associated with the social license

This relationship is expressed in Figure 2.1. I very much see the social license as a modern manifestation of much older ideas—particularly those expressed in social contract theory over the past 200–300 years.

Whilst sufficient legitimacy, trust, and consent are preconditions for the social license to exist (examined further in the second part of this book), a wider range of contextual factors might help to explain what causes the social license to improve or deteriorate (the third part of this book), as expressed in Figure 2.1. These factors present specific opportunities and challenges for the different organizations involved (examined in the final part of this book).

In very simple terms, to build and maintain their social license for an activity, organizations need to ensure that they do not undermine the pre-existing social contract within a given society and that they are in harmony with it. It starts to get tricky in situations where the social contract is weak or already undermined by a corrupt, rent-seeking elite or where civil society itself is weak, disempowered, and divided. So organizations need to think about the social contract in international terms. They need to assess whether the existing social contract measures up to internationally recognized norms—and in particular internationally recognized human rights—as the touchstone for gaining and maintaining license.

Licenses to operate (legal, political, social)

I do not see social license in isolation from the array of other relationships that organizations have with each other regarding particular activities. When trying to understand the social license, it is useful to consider two other interrelated "licenses" that sit alongside it, the more traditional "legal" and "political" licenses. As Figure 2.2 below suggests, all three are increasingly interdependent in the modern world.

Political

If the organization is a government, then its legitimacy is derived from the social contract, as expressed by the electorate, from a state's constitution, and/or from a head of state. Political license thus is the authority that the government gives to any other organization to undertake a particular activity. In many societies where governments have been authoritarian it is the only form of license that has really mattered. If you have the

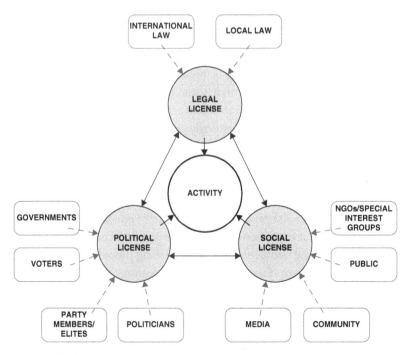

FIG 2.2 ╱ Political, legal, and social license

blessing of the political elite, then the granting of a legal license is a mere formality; and who worries about social license if the population is living in fear of the army or police? But the world does not quite work like this nowadays—unless you live in North Korea. Even some of the most powerful governments in the world find that they need more than political license for specific activities that might be controversial with particular sections of their population. So whilst governments are the duty-bearers in social contract terms, with the right to use armed force if necessary, they too are increasingly interested in social license.

Legal

Businesses and other legal institutions and organizations require a legal license to operate. Sometimes the organization will be non-profit-making; at other times profits will be required for shareholders, or for employees (in the case of a partnership) or customers (in the case of a cooperative). Legal license matters a lot: no non-state organization wants to operate illegally unless it is happy to be criminalized. But as the earlier quote from Bruce Harvey affirms, a piece of paper from a government authority is often not enough for an activity to proceed.

There are still many legal loopholes around the world, either because the law or regulation is missing or because it is not implemented. So, it is very important to be clear that social license should not fill the void left by the lack of political will to create a stronger legal license. However, even when the legal license is strongly applied by the state to non-state organizations, such as business, it is still not always enough to ensure that the organization is carrying out its activities in ways that do not have significant negative social impacts. If health and safety or environmental regulation were still stronger in the USA than they are today, would the BP Gulf of Mexico disaster have been avoided? Perhaps yes, perhaps no. Even the strongest regulation we have in the world will not stop the global demand for natural resources or companies taking (hopefully well judged) risks to exploit them. Even if we take the position that for reasons of climate change, all new coal, oil, and gas reserves should be left untouched, there will still be hazardous industries of other kinds (fishing and logging are still much more dangerous professions for those who work in these industries). The risk of disasters such as that in the Gulf of Mexico can hopefully be reduced still further through better regulation, but it cannot be eliminated completely. Fundamentally, governments, businesses, and other types of organization have to explain their risks and their decision-making to wider groups in society, so that the risks are better understood and that communities feel they have a stake in the decisions made. Hence the need for a better understanding of social license.

There are different types of social group, including the public, media, and NGOs/special interest groups. Social license is strongest, or weakest, when the interests of all of these categories are aligned in favor of or against an activity. However, very often they are not fully aligned. For example, a company might have the support of the majority of a local community, yet not the national or international NGOs, or the media might be critical of a policy or a project that many in the general public are apathetic about and so on. It is critical when considering the social license not to regard all social groups as a homogeneous entity. For the purpose of this book "special interest groups" is widely defined to include lobby groups, religious organizations, investors (including socially responsible investors), political parties, and so on. Almost by definition, there will nearly always be a minority of special interest groups not aligned with other social groups in relation to the social license for any controversial activity.

Social license must be understood in relation to the social contract

As I have pointed out, the social license is so important because many activities will be continually challenged by a range of actors in society, from communities to NGOs, media to the wider society. But no one can fully appreciate its significance in today's world, understanding it in the context of 300 years of thinking about how society grants legitimacy and consent to specific activities carried out on their behalf.

Despite contemporary interest in the social license, it is only now that academic, business, and civil society literature has started to link the concept to longer-standing traditions—particularly that of the "social contract" espoused by Thomas Hobbes, John Locke, Jean-Jacques Rousseau, and others in the 17th and 18th centuries.[18] The idea of a social contract threw away the idea of "divine right"—the belief that rulers gained their legitimacy directly from God and needed no other. A social contract was an explicit or tacit agreement between the ruler and the ruled. In its crudest form, the *Leviathan* espoused by Hobbes,[19] a powerful ruler would provide security and the protection of rights, in exchange for allowing the ruled to enjoy a range of fundamental freedoms and rights. This idea was refined by Locke[20] and Rousseau[21] into contract theories more familiar to modern theories of democracy: the ruled surrender a number of rights and freedoms to the ruler in exchange for the protections required for all other rights to be enjoyed. For Locke this meant a democratically elected government. For Rousseau it was the direct involvement of the public in decision-making. I will explore this thinking more deeply, in particular in relation to ideas of *consent*. Arguably, of the three, it was Rousseau who came closest to modern ideas of social license.

Much of what has been written on social contracts has been focused on the relationship between the state and the individual, and ideas such as democracy and human rights have been central to this. Arguably, social contract theory has only in recent decades received renewed attention through the work of John Rawls and others, and through applications such as "game theory" to explain negotiating, problem-solving, and other behaviors. One explicit application to non-state organizations has been the work of Tom Donaldson and others on Integrative Social Contract Theory in relation to business ethics. This brings into focus social norms, such as internationally recognized human rights, into decision-making structures between international companies and local communities, showing the complexity and contradictions within ethical approaches.[22]

Similarly, my contention is that social license can therefore be seen as a contemporary manifestation of social contract theory. Putting it in such a historical context can be helpful in highlighting some of the underlying tensions that are as current today as they were 250 years ago, as well as contemporary challenges resulting from globalization. Doing so raises a number of initial issues.

First, social license is potentially a profound concept if seen as a type of social contract with implications for all societal actors. As Kant argued, the social contract is a premise for the existence of civil society itself— including the search for an international civil society, which Kant felt was humanity's greatest challenge.[23]

Therefore, it would be too limiting to think of a business striving to achieve its social license within the backdrop of a uniform and aligned "social sphere." Rather, community organizations and NGOs themselves are constantly striving to achieve and renew their own social licenses—business is just one of these, albeit an often very well resourced, well networked, and powerful social actor. Even as late as the mid-1990s some were still defining businesses as NGOs (and in fact Paul Polman, the CEO of Unilever, still jokes that he leads the world's largest NGO).[24] For the purposes of social license arguments, however, it is important to distinguish between three types of social actor: state actors who classically bear the duties invested in them by the social contract, non-state actors with a primary social purpose, and non-state actors whose primary purpose is non-social. Later in this book I will ask, as Paul Polman suggests, whether there really is such a thing as a business whose primary purpose is social. Certainly, when I worked at The Body Shop International the founders of the company saw its purpose as being as much social as financial, but the City of London—where the company was listed—never really saw it that way. The test for Unilever will come when it is not returning healthy profits. Can a business afford to maintain strong social commitments if markets do not reward them for doing so? It might be that we are indeed on the verge of a new era of shared value, but what would this mean in social license terms?

A second observation is that a social contract is never permanent, and, like social license, it is a dynamic relationship. The philosopher Guizot argued against Rousseau, stating: "What does it matter if a law should have emanated from my will yesterday if today my will has changed? Can I only will once? Does my will exhaust its rights in one single act?"[25] This reminds us that as long as there have been arguments about social contracts there have also been arguments about their permanency.

In terms of law-making, this is perhaps less problematic; laws can be developed or reversed in keeping with the values and expectations of society. How this might happen with social license is more obscure. Central to this is the idea of *consent,* which will be examined later in this book. What is important to remember here is that *consent* is not a single decision point: *consent* can be reversed or consent can be lost. For companies or governments investing hundreds of millions of dollars in a specific project, the need to maintain *consent* is paramount. Obviously, extremists would argue that guns and bullets are one option for overriding the tiresome *consent* issue, bribes and co-option of local opposition still others. However, I am more interested in how social license can be maintained through consent that has been freely given and also that is fully informed of the choices available. This brief reflection of the wider philosophical context reminds us that there is nothing new about the tension between free will, which might reach different conclusions at different times, and the consent required for social license.

A third observation is also a fundamental criticism of the legitimacy of the contracting process itself. In essence, the social contract is a facet of liberalism and therefore one of co-option of less powerful interests by elitism. A Marxist interpretation might argue that much social contract theory is about maintaining the status quo and legitimizing existing hegemonic relationships in society. Much of the anti-globalization movement and contemporary approaches to corporate accountability, for example, would raise the same concern. In whose interests are the contracts framed? Is the weaker party giving only tacit and not active consent to the arrangement?

My contention is that if social license is indeed a serious concept, and a contemporary form of social contract, then all related concepts are worthy of exploration. This is no tick-box approach, rather an articulation of something complex: how any organization can legitimately engage in the lives of others.

Local social license is not an absolute

Society is not a homogeneous entity—local communities are not always in line with regional or national opinion, particularly when a specific activity has local impacts. Therefore the absence of local social license does not necessarily mean an activity is illegitimate in the eyes of wider society. The withholding of local social license, therefore, is not always a socially progressive force—it can sometimes be reactionary. For example, it is not always about protecting the rights of marginalized and vulnerable groups against a powerful majority. Rich people in the countryside, for example, may also seek to deny social license by thwarting any attempts to build social housing or create jobs for working people. The point is best made here, early in the book, that local social license is not a new panacea for social justice or human rights activism. Local social interests should be afforded no absolute "trump card" over wider dimensions of social license; otherwise we risk privileging Nimbyism (the "Not In My Back Yard" sentiment), as will be discussed in Chapter 6. One exception is the particular rights of indigenous peoples. Yet even here the absence of consent is not an absolute veto against all development, even if the absence of local consent is the absence of any meaningful social license in local terms. So organizations need to consider social license in local, regional, and national terms. When these are not aligned, it is only careful analysis—and reference to international norms such as human rights—that will help define legitimate actions, even if some in society are not in agreement.

Communities are instinctively concerned about the "new" or the "other." Yet people are also excited and intrigued by these same things. The human condition is a complex one riven with contradictions and competing demands. Therefore, social license sits at the confluence of a number of archetypes that often come into conflict with each other. What might seem to be fundamental contradictions between social, legal, or political licenses might not always be so on closer examination. International legal norms, such as internationally recognized human rights, can play a central role in clarifying the correct medium-to-long-term arc of decision making outside of the context of short-term pressures and lobbying from specific interest groups.

Governments, businesses, and NGOs can still choose to ignore or override the social license, even in situations when it would be foolhardy to do so. Short-term interests still, too often, prevail. Powerful organizations in many situations can still enforce their will through political or legal license—let's not pretend otherwise—even though the contexts for doing so might be diminishing. I contend that whilst social license is an emerging and important consideration for all organizations, it is still an emerging priority, but one that will become an implacable reality.

The social license in a nutshell

So the key take-away points from this chapter are:

1. The social license relates to the activities of any organization. It cannot be directly managed or self-awarded; rather, it is the accumulation of a number of factors, which will be explored in greater depth later in this book. It is these factors that organizations can manage, not the social license itself.

2. It is much easier to notice the absence of social license than its presence. The presence of social license might be described as an equitable balance, or harmony, between different interests that allows an activity to continue and to thrive. However, as it is dynamic, it can always be withdrawn.
3. The social license relates to what an organization *does* as opposed to what it *is*—i.e. it relates to the activities of an organization.
4. The social license should be understood in social contract terms and therefore different types of organization will acquire social license in different ways for their activities because they have a different relationship to the social contract. The classic distinctions are: for governments, by being accountable and effective servants of the social contract in society; for civil society, by strengthening the accountability of government or the strength of the social contract itself; and for business (whose primary purpose is not social) by not weakening the social contact or exploiting existing weaknesses, but by finding ways of building capacity within the existing social contract without replacing it. Later in this book, I will test this hypothesis, as there is evidence that on some issues, such as internet governance, dealing with remote communities or international public–private partnerships, business is being granted a much wider social license and treated as if it were a social actor such as an NGO or even a government.
5. The social license does not replace political license or legal license; in fact quite the opposite is the case. However, both legal and political licenses have limitations and they are increasingly reliant on the social license.
6. The limitations of existing political and legal license need to be understood in an international context and against international norms such as human rights. Modern interpretations of social contract theory have made much use of human rights and so too does this approach to understanding social license.

3

What's wrong with CSR?

"[CSR] implies that business ... has no inherent social utility, but requires a sanitising 'add-on'—something which enables it to 'give back' to society, a sentiment frequently heard on the lips of corporate leaders apparently unaware that this suggests that their own core activities are parasitic, which, without appropriate policies and principles relating to the whole of their impact, they may indeed be."

Sir Geoffrey Chandler (2003)[1]

Corporate social responsibility (CSR) has grown into a global industry, with companies and CEOs lining up to show how they contribute social and environmental value to some of society's most pressing problems. This, of course, is a good thing—better than the Milton Friedman vision of business operating in a context totally removed from society.[2] CSR has undoubtedly made a positive contribution. The issue is that there is much that currently sits under the umbrella of CSR, from self-serving public relations to philanthropy, and from supply chain compliance to working on shared social value projects. So asking a question such as "do you think CSR is a good thing?" is like asking "do you think newspapers are a good thing?"—it depends a lot on the content. This diversity of things that are included under the CSR banner, and the lack of a clear definition, means that the label "CSR" is not helpful because it too often obscures rather than clarifies any activity's relationship with the social contract. In other words CSR as a concept often does not always connect the way the "C" (corporation) might be constrained by the "S" (social) in terms of societal expectations.

As we consider such concerns with current understandings of CSR it is important to hold in our minds an important caveat. As the growing CSR movement has taken most of the oxygen at the business–society interface for several years, many important initiatives have chosen to use the CSR label for reasons of expediency or pragmatism. We needed to find a label of some kind. My purpose is to show something of the conceptual gap that needs to be filled if we are to explore the social responsibilities of non-state actors seriously and the value the social license concept might offer in this context. For anyone who might find some of my criticisms of CSR a little too direct, remember that I am criticizing myself here also—I have worked in CSR for nearly 20 years. My intention is to point to where I see problems and offer a way forward.

CSR lacks a clear definition, purpose, or end goal

There are many definitions of CSR. Sometimes, when I am teaching, I put on the PowerPoint presentation the official (but unattributed) CSR definitions recognized by the Brazilian, Chinese, and Indian governments, as well as that of the European Union, to see if the students can guess which belongs to whom. It is a fun exercise—try it sometime, perhaps for the whole of the G20. The idea of business doing good for society has been interpreted in line with the political context of each of these economies and the societies they reflect. There is no internationally recognized definition of CSR. Even the United Nations does not have a common definition between its agencies. The following is used by the United Nations Industrial Development Organization (UNIDO):

> Corporate Social Responsibility is a management concept whereby companies integrate social and environmental concerns in their business operations and interactions with their stakeholders.[3]

This definition seems to be fairly representative of the status quo. When CSR is defined at all it is usually defined as a business management concept and focuses very much on its operational utility from a business perspective. Not surprisingly, CSR as currently understood often does not give any sense of why any other organization, which is not a business, should engage in the CSR concept—nor why those deemed to be "stakeholders" should also wish to engage.

In 2011, the European Commission revised its own definition and now has much more of a societal purpose to it:

> [social responsibility is] the responsibility of enterprises for their impacts on society. To fully meet their social responsibility, enterprises should have in place a process to integrate social, environmental, ethical, human rights and consumer concerns into their business operations and core strategy in close collaboration with their stakeholders.[4]

There are indications that other governments are also looking to "reclaim CSR" from purely being a business management concept. The OECD position since 2011 has been:

> Corporate responsibility involves the search for an effective "fit" between businesses and the societies in which they operate. The notion of "fit" recognizes the mutual dependence of business and society—a business sector cannot prosper if the society in which it operates is failing and a failing business sector inevitably detracts from general wellbeing. "Corporate responsibility" refers to the actions taken by businesses to nurture and enhance this symbiotic relationship.[5]

It should be noted that the OECD explicitly does not use the CSR term, suggesting to me, at least, that they too may see its limitations and lack of societal focus. Whilst neither the EU nor the OECD definition explicitly references the social contract, they clearly embody some of what Hobbes, Rousseau, and Kant espoused: whilst not directly part of civil society, business is closely related to it and its impacts can have a profound effect upon society as a whole. In other words, business can have both a positive or negative impact on the social contract that binds together society itself and the relationship between governments and the governed.

These developments have been influenced by renewed efforts in the UN system to better clarify business responsibilities in the area of human rights. Both the EU and OECD positions reflect the work done during the mandate of the UN Special Representative on Business and Human Rights which Professor John Ruggie undertook between 2005 and 2011. The UN

Guiding Principles on Business and Human Rights, the outcome of John Ruggie's work, have also been adopted by other organizations such as the ISO, whose 26,000 standard is popular amongst businesses in over 70 countries.[6]

Human rights mean all those rights recognized internationally since the 1948 Universal Declaration of Human Rights and the two UN Human Rights Covenants, which together form "The International Bill of Human Rights." Given that all the world's governments already recognize these rights (in theory if not always in practice), it is fitting that any global approach to the social responsibilities of business places these responsibilities in the same framework as the pre-existing duties of governments. Therefore, John Ruggie's "Protect, Respect, Remedy" framework—issued in 2008—does just this. His UN Guiding Principles on Business and Human Rights were endorsed by governments in June 2011 and shows both governments and businesses how best to start to implement their respective duties and responsibilities. I will refer to human rights a lot in this book, particularly because the UN Guiding Principles is a clear example of how the social impacts of an organization, in this case business, can be considered alongside those of government. In social license terms this makes perfect sense and in particular if we follow social contract thinking: government is in itself the servant of the social contract that binds society itself. If greater clarity about the societal purpose of CSR is emerging, thanks to internationally agreed norms such as the UN Guiding Principles on Business and Human Rights, there remains less about its ultimate goal. Here governments will turn to how CSR aligns with existing sustainability goals (such as those on climate change) or development goals (in particular the 2000–15 United Nations Millennium Development Goals—MDGs). This is a good response—even if a little after the fact—as the role of business in achieving the MDGs has been a bit of an afterthought of the 2000 MDGs, perhaps less so when their replacement is agreed in 2015. But what fundamentally is the purpose of CSR?

If governments see CSR as a way of leveraging business support for their own national and international agendas, this is not quite the way it is perceived within business and many parts of civil society. Many in civil society still believe CSR is essentially about the self-legitimization of what are increasingly powerful (and some would argue at times unaccountable) corporate actors, who find themselves as powerful drivers of current economic globalization. This is not quite my own view, but it is justifiable criticism of what still might be described as parts of mainstream CSR.

Having worked in business, civil society, and with governments and UN agencies, I get the feeling that there is good intent on many parts to try to make the jigsaw fit together. The problem is that CSR has been shaped in such a way that it does not fit the hole required of it. A term which ranges from philanthropic gestures such as building hospitals or sponsoring local football teams all the way through to building the capacity of suppliers or local governments is too broad and too shallow. The unfortunate reality is that CSR has become a conceptual sideshow and a conceptual ceiling at the same time—sometimes distracting attention from the most important social impacts a company has and other times, even when a company is focusing on its core impacts, encouraging companies to determine on their own how they relate to wider society. For example, CSR might encourage a pharmaceutical company to focus on overtime issues in its supply chain more than on a robust discussion about access to medicines, lobbying, and patent rights—this is the "sideshow" or offsetting from its largest social impacts. Even if the company does see access to its products as its CSR priority, it might still approach the issue in a business-centric way, defining its own limits in isolation and not fully embracing the perspectives of patients, doctors, health services, and those who cannot afford the medicine but are in the greatest need.

"CSR has become a conceptual sideshow and a conceptual ceiling at the same time"

The absence of an agreed global definition of CSR has not helped, and now there is so much organizational investment in various definitions of the concept that conceptually CSR is more of a hindrance than an asset—until the time a common definition is agreed. The United Nations Guiding Principles on Business and Human Rights gives us a consensus that it is the impact on people that matters the most, the responsibility of non-state actors—such as companies—needs to be understood from the perspective of society itself, and in particular the most marginalized and vulnerable communities and individuals, upon whom a negative impact can be greatest.

CSR is not core to the business model

CSR has been attacked as a concept not just by civil society but also by some in business itself, or at least those who think about business a lot. The *Economist* magazine has for many years criticized CSR as being something of a sideshow and a distraction. Anyone who has worked in a company will know what this means. The Director of Procurement, Sales, Marketing, or Operations often ask, "what does this mean to me? Is this a serious part of what I have to do to meet my targets and to drive the business forward?" And the honest answer, even for many companies with glossy CSR reports, is "no, not really." When push comes to shove, business unit managers in many companies are rarely fired for not meeting CSR targets (unless they are the CSR manager themselves). They might be marked down on their scorecard during appraisal, but not fired. However, if they seriously breached health and safety, workplace discrimination, or the personal privacy of an employee, they might well be fired—and rightly so. But this is often not seen as CSR? Many of my CSR colleagues in companies have bemoaned the fact that they are not able to influence directly the way workers are treated in their own company; this sits with the human resources function which is not always aligned with the CSR team.

Herein lies the contradiction in the way many businesses still regard CSR. If CSR is too often seen only as what is voluntary, then it is always on the edge of what one must do. This understanding of CSR would imply that because health and safety or equal opportunities are something one must do, then they can't be part of the CSR function. But why would some of the most serious social impacts a company can have not be seen as corporate social responsibility? It is a responsibility, it is social, and it is most definitely within a corporation.

At the United Nations in 2011 John Ruggie called for an end to "self-declaratory CSR" and some such as the EU and OECD listened. But "old style" CSR continues to live on, with its never-ending CEO conferences and roadshows. But underneath the CSR fluff there are a number of more substantive trends emerging. The fact that much of what is referred to today as CSR has had little to do with core business has been recognized for a long time, and now even the likes of Michael Porter and Mark Kramer are talking about CSR or the need for an improved version of it.[7] So whilst civil society has criticized CSR for its lack of accountability, business schools have criticized it for its lack of focus on innovation and the creation of value. The concept of "shared value" is a compelling one and has attracted the attention of a number of leading CEOs. The concept of shared value can be defined as: "policies and operating practices that enhance the competitiveness of a company while simultaneously advancing the economic and social conditions in the communities in which it operates."

The role of business innovation in terms of tackling societal ills, in particular in healthcare, or the opportunities brought to the world by the internet and mobile telephones, suggests that there is much that shared value can deliver as a concept. If the "shared value" construct helps to bring CSR closer to core business models, then this is a good thing also. But if business is serious about contributing proactively to the social and economic conditions of communities, as Porter and Kramer suggest, it is then closer to impacting on the social contract. What is missing from much of the discussion on shared value are the consent-based and justice-based expectations we might have for businesses. As I will seek to explain, true shared value will not be possible without social license.

"shared value will not be possible without social license"

Why social license might be a more useful concept

The EU and OECD definitions of corporate responsibility now give a stronger emphasis to the interests of society, but they still rest on a number of assumptions:

- That businesses can be made, or incentivized, to manage their social impacts not for their benefit but for the benefit of society;
- That when the interests of society or a specific community conflict with the commercial interests of a business, businesses will consistently and voluntarily defer to the social interest even if they are not required by law to do so;
- That when needed, governments will be willing to regulate to compel businesses to act in the interests of society and not their own;
- That governments and politicians can be trusted to reflect the interests of the whole of society, including the most marginalized people.

Ideas such as shared value look at "win-win" possibilities. Much less attention in CSR is given to "lose-win" or "win-lose" scenarios. It is gratifying when civil society organizations, business, and governments can all sit around a table and agree on the need for binding regulation relating to a societal ill such as conflict minerals, human trafficking, and forced labor, or the activities of labor brokers. But there are many more cases where current business imperatives are not well aligned with the long-term interests of society and these discussions normally take the form of "naming and shaming reports," lawsuits, threats of libel action, and so on, rather than robust but respectful discussion about what really can be done based on the interests of all concerned. However, regulation often does not work like this, sometimes business will lobby hard against legislation that is in the wider interests of society (think, for example, of those corporate lobby groups which fought hard against restrictions to smoking advertising, environmental protections, or even climate change). Too often CSR struggles to address such contradictions by overlooking those areas where the short-term interests of business are not aligned with the longer-term interests of society. Companies will always operate out of self-interest—there is nothing wrong with this—but equally a more impartial understanding of the business–society interface is needed than the one CSR often brings.

So to close this section, let's recap on why social license might be a more useful concept than CSR for any organization when trying to define what is going on, and what will need to go on for organizations to be responsible societal actors. In my opinion, social license offers the following advantages:

- It describes the set of relationships between a given organization (business, government agency, or whatever) and individuals and communities in society. Non-state actors need to be clear about whether they are part of the social contract (i.e. civil society) or not (i.e. organizations whose primary purpose is not social), and then interact on social issues accordingly.
- Unlike CSR, social license relates to specific activities and not to organizations. Therefore it avoids platitudes such as "company x is good at CSR" or "company y is a good company."
- Social license cannot be "self-declared"—it describes an equitable balance of interests which allows an activity to continue and to thrive, but it is dynamic and can always be withdrawn. Organizations can

work to achieve the underpinning requirements, the result of which will hopefully be social license. But social license cannot be managed or controlled directly by *any* organization. This also reflects the reality that even a local community cannot necessarily hold the right to veto a particular activity if it is clearly in the interests of all others.

• Social license avoids tiresome generalities about whether mandatory or voluntary approaches to CSR are better. Social license focuses on the impacts of specific activities and the associated behavior of all involved. By focusing on the outcomes, it allows discussions about how best to get there—what needs to be required by law and what does not.

The end of CSR?

Well, not quite. I hope my opinions here are taken for what they are: a long look in the mirror at the current state of CSR. If the CSR label can be reclaimed and invested more consistently with something much more legitimate in social terms, then long live CSR. I am not as eloquent or strident as Sir Geoffrey Chandler (whose quote opened this chapter), but many of us who cut our teeth on business and human rights in the 1990s owe much to Geoffrey and his chairing of Amnesty International UK's Business Group (and also to Chris Marsden, now Chair of Trustees for both my own organization and the Business and Human Rights Resource Centre). Geoffrey could not abide CSR. Even 15 to 20 years ago, he smelled a rat. His razor-sharp intellect saw that the conceptual premises upon which CSR was being built were the wrong ones—and this from a man who had served for most of his life as a senior executive in Shell Oil. It is perhaps because he had been educated in both philosophy and international business that he was passionate on the issue. Whether we need CSR or not is still an open question, but the world certainly needs more Geoffreys.

Part **2**

The Foundations

4

Legitimacy

Which organizations might receive social license for their activities?

"The strongest is never strong enough to be always the master, unless he transforms strength into right, and obedience into duty."[1]

Jean-Jacques Rousseau (1762)

As already observed, it is much easier for an organization to see when it does not have social license for a specific activity than when it does. These next three chapters explore three concepts: *legitimacy*, *trust*, and *consent*, which are, in my view at least, prerequisites for any discussion about whether an activity has social license or not. They are preconditions in a definitional sense. As no organization can award itself a social license for an activity, it comes by understanding the activity's relationship with the pre-existing social contract, then it must hold true that both the organization and activity in question are sufficiently legitimate, are trusted enough, and that the communities and/or wider population in question have consented to the said activity.

This chapter explores perhaps the most central concept that relates to the social license: *legitimacy*. It is a tricky one to define, let alone measure, and assessments of who or what is legitimate will vary according to who is asked. However, this chapter comes early in the book for a reason: I believe that obtaining social license for an activity is impossible without some level of organizational legitimacy as well as legitimacy for the activity in question. In other words, both the actor and the action need to be sufficiently legitimate.

Although the words *law* and *legitimacy* share a common root in Latin, it is clear that today they mean different things. Whilst obeying the law is normally key to a government or company's legitimacy, sometimes national laws will conflict with norms of international law and therefore not be legitimate in the eyes of the international community. Think of the laws passed during the time of colonization or totalitarianism in Europe during the 20th century for example. Whilst it was not illegal for most international companies to trade with apartheid South Africa, was it ever legitimate for them to do so? This is a point that is still discussed today, more than 20 years after the release of Nelson Mandela.

It is clear that international law, whilst it has little punitive effect on nation states, except perhaps in the realm of trade law, does matter a great deal to issues of organizational legitimacy. Alleged breaches of international law are often cited by governments when seeking to justify intervening in the internal affairs of another state. Election results are held up or ignored on the basis of the (il)legitimacy of the processes involved. It is noticeable how much US politicians used the term before both of the Gulf Wars, and how often it was used by the leaders of the Palestinian state around the time of the UN vote which recognized its existence in the eyes of most other states. Legitimacy is the social mechanism used by political elites to maintain their power base and justify many of their actions. Law can be aligned with legitimacy but sometimes it is not—law correcting the excesses of a powerful elite or legitimacy used to justify ignoring or striking down old laws. In the rapid decision-making environment of the modern world, it is norms of legitimacy in the eyes of the public that guide and constrain policymakers, as much as the law itself—the law often taking time to catch up.[2]

The challenges with legitimacy as a concept

One problem from the outset is methodological. Legitimacy is not a directly observable phenomenon: it exists only in the eye of the beholder. As a sentiment it is not only hard to record, but also highly subjective, operating at both a conscious and an unconscious level.[3] However, the legitimacy of governments and non-state actors such as businesses is a widespread global concern that can move populations on the streets as much as to the ballot box. It is also not a concept new to academics or those who write about different types of organization.

Businesses notoriously only like concepts they can measure ("what can be counted can be managed"). The lack of objectivity, lack of measurability, and the blatantly political nature of the concept all add up to making legitimacy a difficult idea to weave into the CEO's speech or annual report. If there is one thing likely to "scare the horses," it will be a CEO talking about legitimacy. Yet, it is a concept that business is absorbing by osmosis, if not by design. The clever business strategists of course understand the concept well. Even if it will not appear in public statements, it is the essence of much Boardroom talk. Now that Michael Porter from the Harvard Business School is using the "L" word, it is only a matter of time before it becomes mainstream.[4] As Charles Green writes:

> There is no "legitimacy index," and any attempt at mapping something as ephemeral as legitimacy will be fraught with subjectivity. But let me suggest a commonsensical outline. Legitimacy broadly tracks such social phenomena as trust and confidence, heroes vs. villains, and the popularity of going into business as a career choice. By these indicia, the socially perceived legitimacy of business was low in the 1960s, high in the '80s, and is at a nadir now.[5]

Although a government can draw its legitimacy from its sovereignty, the will or self-determination of its people, and its recognition in the eyes of other states or bodies such as the United Nations, for non-state actors there is no such formal process of legitimization. It is not just businesses that have to worry about legitimacy; other non-state actors such as NGOs, trade unions, community groups, armed rebels, and religious groups need to as well. Indeed, for non-state actors the question is even more important. It is in fact *the* question: in whose interest does the organization purport to operate and in what ways is it accountable to that constituency?

Sufficient organizational legitimacy is a prerequisite for social license

As already stated, one precondition for social license is that both the organization and the specific activity need to have an adequate level of legitimacy. A legitimate organization cannot expect that all its activities will be seen as legitimate, and an illegitimate organization cannot hope that it will gain legitimacy by carrying out what would otherwise be seen as legitimate activities. Not all of Al Capone's activities were illegitimate, but because his organization was, then so were they.

There are four ways in which the legitimacy of an organization and an activity can relate. The first of these, where both the organization and activity are perceived as illegitimate, is dismissed here in social license terms. Take the international arms, drugs, or human trafficking industries as an extreme case—illegitimate (and also illegal). I will not focus any pages of this book on discussing how criminal organizations might achieve some level of societal legitimacy (albeit sometimes they do in remote or heavily marginalized communities). Instead, I will examine the three other scenarios: when the organization or the activity is sufficiently legitimate, and cases when they both are.

Scenario one: Sufficient legitimacy for an activity but insufficient legitimacy for the organization(s)

Let's take the example of a tobacco grower which treats its field workers well and provides jobs in an otherwise poor area of Central Asia. The fact that they have worked hard to eliminate child labor, for example, might be seen as indication that their local social license for their supply chain activity is legitimizing their business model more generally. But this would be misleading, for those who oppose smoking on health grounds around the world (and let's face it, this is becoming a majority in many countries), the fact that child labor is being eradicated in the global supply chain matters little in terms of gaining legitimacy for what is increasingly seen as an illegitimate industry. For the tobacco company to try to promote its legitimacy by claiming that it has a local social license creates an immediate tension between the different social licenses for each of its activities—local communities in the supply chain versus the production and marketing of the product. The absence of international legitimacy has increasingly restricted the social license of tobacco companies in many of their historic markets to advertise, to market, and to sell (no longer can they associate their brands with otherwise "healthy" sports). The industry cannot truly claim to have strong social license and the fact that it might have local license within some communities is not the same as its having more general social license for all its activities; nor does it answer questions of organizational legitimacy.

Scenario two: Sufficient legitimacy for the organization(s) but insufficient legitimacy for its activity

Let's now consider the arrival of US troops in Iraq to overthrow an oppressive government. Whilst the occupying troops might enjoy some element of social license for their activities in certain communities initially—particularly if they are able to protect local populations—their activities will almost always not been seen as legitimate over the longer term. They are, at the end of the day, invaders—even if operating through the best of intentions from their perspective. This is very different from questioning the legitimacy of the United States Army itself—as a sovereign power the United States has a legitimate right to protect itself and its interests, within the bounds of international law.

This lack of legitimacy for the activity will undermine the US Army's social license if there is not a clear exit strategy or a handover to others more legitimate in the context. Of course, the occupying troops might choose to stay without any social license, but they will need to enforce their presence through political or legal license in order to do so. This is similar to discussions in the UK on largely unarmed, consent-based policing. Without any social license for their activities, the British police could still operate but there would need to be more of them and they would all need to be armed. The policing example also shows how, whilst the legitimacy of the existence of a police force itself is rarely questioned (although it has been historically in Northern Ireland or in the investigations into cover-ups such as after the Hillsborough disaster), most people in society will question the legitimacy of specific police-related activities. If a police force routinely carries out activities that a community feels are illegitimate, such as "stop and search" actions in largely black or Asian areas of London, then its social license will be threatened. Senior police leaders know this, even if they do not routinely use the language of the social contract or the social license.

Scenario three: Sufficient legitimacy for both the organization(s) and the activity

Scenario three is the sweet spot—one in which both the organization or organizations involved and the activity in question are sufficiently legitimate. It is in the interests of most organizations to achieve this, of course, and huge amounts of public information, media control, and advertising, brand management, campaigning, and so forth are focused on this goal—maintaining and promoting the legitimacy of both the organization itself and what it does. Scenario three might then be assumed to be the default state, the basis for most organizational relationships that exist around the world as well as for the way that organizations relate to individual people.

The challenge, of course, is that every organization—of whatever type—will claim to be legitimate and will claim that whatever activity it has an interest in is also legitimate. Others will sometimes see things differently but might always explicitly concur for a whole host of reasons ranging from politeness to corruption, fear of legal repercussions, and even personal safety. So, most often, the question about whether a business, an NGO, or even a government is truly legitimate is asked only by academics, activists, or journalists. Organizations tend to think these things but not say them. Yet any attempt to develop social license in a context where, for example, a business feels that a community group is not really legitimate, or the community feels that the business itself is not legitimate, or either party feels that the proposed activity should not really be going ahead, will fail unless the dialog itself reveals things otherwise unknown.

Dialog, transparency, and knowledge can clearly improve perceptions of legitimacy, but there is also a deeper core to the question.

An NGO might say, for example, that it is not engaging in dialog with a business purely because it is a for-profit enterprise and therefore intrinsically untrustworthy. This is an extreme view, and one held only by a minority of NGOs. However, it is not likely to be conducive to the social

"organizational views on which other organizations are legitimate or not, can and must be mediated by objective norms based in international law"

license if local communities and other social groups also think in this way. Similarly, one organization might refuse to work with another due to a range of illegitimate factors—ranging from its social status or the gender, ethnicity, sexual orientation, religion, or political views of its members. Therefore, organizational views as to which other organizations are legitimate or not, can and must be mediated by objective norms based in international law in order to obviate prejudicial views of legitimacy from whichever perspective they come. Thus perceptions of legitimacy need to be contested, to be aired publicly, and to be challenged.

Legitimacy and NGOs

Let's take for a moment the example of some of the best-known global NGOs. On the environmental side of things, how would Friends of the Earth define its organizational legitimacy compared with, say, Greenpeace International? The former has a membership which is represented at the national and international level, and it makes decisions along democratic lines. On the other hand, Greenpeace does not have members, but supporters (who donate, but have no vote on how the NGO should run itself). In fact, the joke used to be that Greenpeace was the only NGO with its own navy accountable only to five people in Amsterdam. Does the fact that Friends of the Earth has a membership structure make it more legitimate than Greenpeace? Some would say yes, but some would disagree, saying that Greenpeace is still accountable to its donors, who support the NGO on the basis of its willingness to take risks.

There is a similar division among human rights NGOs—with the "democratic" Amnesty International on the one hand and the more "top-down" Human Rights Watch on the other. How do these NGOs define and safeguard their own legitimacy? Both are acutely aware that the days are numbered when global NGOs can mainly be supported by rich white people pointing their fingers at problems that are mainly in the global South. Unless they can claim to be truly global in their governance and not just in terms of their campaigns, they risk losing their legitimacy. As mentioned already, for NGOs—and in particular campaigning NGOs— their perceived legitimacy is their most precious asset.[6]

Another non-state example is that of religious groups. Here the complexity comes from the fact that most religions draw their legitimacy directly from the god or gods that the religion worships. This is a self-defining legitimacy and not necessarily one recognized by believers of other faiths or those of no faith at all. Self-proclaimed legitimacy works within a specific belief system but is challenged when it confronts other such systems, unless some level of harmonization is achieved. Businesses are not unlike religious groups in many ways and have tended to be self-referential in defining their own legitimacy. Read the "values statements" of most companies and you will still see lots of self-referential and subjective proclamations that are often not measurable or comparable with other companies or even different business units of the same firm. Until recently businesses have sought to draw their legitimacy from internal, rather than external, sources: to be true to their own missions rather than to contribute to the objectives of others. However, things have started to shift considerably in recent years.

Legitimacy and business

Non-state actors, such as businesses, have not traditionally worried a great deal about their own legitimacy. Libertarian principles would suggest that a company or NGO should be able to do what it likes, providing it does not infringe upon the rights of others in a significant way. Well, yes, perhaps. However, societies themselves are no longer willing to accept such a laissez-faire position. Take the recent financial crisis and the huge amount of public money that has been thrown at saving the private banking industry in many European countries. Did the banks ever act in an illegal manner? They certainly played the rules of the game as they saw them in the early years of the 21st century. Have they lost the legitimacy required to operate in the laissez-faire manner they had grown used to? Almost certainly they have. In the battle for corporate legitimacy it is perhaps the largest of companies and the dirtiest of industries that have most reason to engage with the concept. A large producer of tobacco, an addictive product with known harmful effects, will need to consider its own legitimacy very carefully. The threat to its social license is fundamental. To a lesser extent, the same is true of any company providing products which are known to be harmful to individuals

(alcoholic, high-sugar, or of poor nutritional value) or
wider communities (the extractive sector), where
the question of legitimacy is central and cannot
be avoided. Is my existence as a company
selling this product to these consumers,
or extracting this raw material from
the ground in this place legitimate?
Companies rarely engage with the question in
these terms, but increasingly they will need to.

"In the battle for corporate legitimacy it's the largest of the companies and the dirtiest of industries that have most reason to engage with the concept"

As Rousseau reminds us in the opening quote of
this chapter, it is the most powerful that most need
to legitimize their hegemony. Therefore, it is perhaps
no coincidence that it is the largest of the world's companies that
have been most active on agendas such as anti-corruption, climate
change, and human rights. Often, this is explained purely in terms of
resources: that large companies have more resources to throw at social
issues. That is too simplistic an explanation for what is really going
on. Large companies know that their future existence as global giants
requires them to behave as global citizens—even if the term is poorly
understood amongst states, let alone amongst non-state actors such as
businesses. Global citizenry requires global rules or norms, and there
has been a tremendous amount of effort spent between governments,
NGOs, and large companies to create such rules. The overarching
motivation for large companies, whether conscious or subconscious, is
the achieving or maintaining of legitimacy in the eyes of social actors
and the public more generally.

Much of the remaining content of this chapter looks at a variety of ways
in which these efforts at legitimization have been taking place. It is central
to understanding social license—in particular, for large companies and/
or those engaged with hazardous, unhealthy, or exploitative products or
industries.

For reasons not dissimilar to those observed by Rousseau 250 years ago,
powerful actors such as large companies need to maintain hegemony by
legitimizing their market positions. Anti-bribery and corruption principles
and standards were one of the first examples of this, followed by climate
change targets and carbon trading, and most recently human rights. As

mentioned before, large companies have engaged in all of these dialogs, usually to develop, sometimes to destroy, not just because they had the resources to do so, but because there is an increasing realization that they are defining their own futures.

Another good example would be the role that large pharmaceutical companies have played, often positive but sometimes not, in public access to medicines. Or the one that mobile telephone companies or internet service providers play in relation to dilemmas on freedom of expression or privacy. These will be explored more deeply later in the book, but suffice it to say for now that aligning an international company with the UN Millennium Development Goals or their successors after 2015 is not just gratuitous philanthropy. There is an element of morality for some of the business leaders involved and, for the companies themselves, the business case is essentially one of legitimacy; legitimacy of their brand, their market share, their profits, their patents, their legacies, and the benefits they accrue by being transnational.

A legitimacy index for business would be a tricky thing to create, and criteria for any such index would shift and then shift again. Nevertheless, some of the battle lines for the debates to come are already being drawn and some are aired here to give you, the reader, something to get your teeth into. Whether or not they will be the true legitimacy tests for every company over the years and decades ahead is unknown. Some of these at least will help to define the legitimacy of business in the 21st century.

What might make a company legitimate?

1. The provision of value

At a minimum, the products and services that a company provides need to be of some extrinsic or intrinsic value to at least someone outside of the company itself. Some companies have taken this further with ideas of "shared value." To put it simply, the firm should add value to the world. Less than legitimate, then, would be the activities of companies whose main purpose was to strip the assets of other companies, parasitical companies, shell companies, and those engaged in fraud, deception, cartels, monopolies, and so on.

2. Understanding its true impacts

Some companies might not be fully aware of the full impact of their operations. For example, a number of apparel companies have in recent years become increasingly aware of how their own purchasing practices (the sometimes last-minute demands they place on the factories that make their clothes around the world) can compel suppliers to subcontract or take on large numbers of temporary staff or migrant laborers. Whilst none of these things are bad in themselves, if they have been undertaken without adequate consideration, the rights of the workers involved might well be at risk. Through the squeezing of global supply chains for cost reductions over many years, the true social cost of producing many clothes has been externalized from the immediate supply chain. The Rana Plaza tragedy in Bangladesh or the factory fires in 2012 in Pakistan and Bangladesh testify to an industry where even basic health and safety can no longer be guaranteed.

Other industries may also not be aware of their true impacts. The misuse of products can take a company by surprise, a pharmaceutical company finds out that one of its drugs is being used as part of a lethal cocktail of products to administer the death penalty in countries such as the USA or China. The dual use of telecommunications equipment is another example. Technology that can locate survivors of an earthquake based on the telephone signals they emit can also be used by a government to locate political dissidents.

As will be argued in Chapter 8, companies can no longer legitimately deny that they did not know or should not have had to know about such risks.

3. The opportunity cost of the company's existence

The scenario is a familiar one even if the cost benefit analysis might be much more complex. For example, a major bookstore moving into a small town where there are already five independent stores, most of which are then put out of business. The net value for the consumers and workers of the town is at best neutral and more likely negative. Similarly, the superstore taking custom away from the high street, or the branded coffee shop chain arriving in a town already well served by good quality independent coffee retailers. A mining operation might bring jobs, oil might bring a new hospital; however, if pollution threatens traditional livelihoods, then the opportunity cost of accepting the business might be high. A business might struggle to be seen as legitimate if its net value is seen to be negative.

4. Efficiency and effective management

A business has to been run effectively and efficiently regardless of how good its social and environmental credentials might be. A profit-sharing cooperative that is run badly might be less legitimate in the eyes of an employee than a profit-making competitor which pays less but promises the worker more security.

5. Company structure, governance, and accountability

Corporate governance has been, for too long, an interest mainly of investors and not of wider society. The fact that only two of the current FTSE 100 companies are led by women, that non-white Board Directors are still under-represented and that the appointments processes to Boards fall far short of being fully open in most cases are becoming wider issues of concern for society. The fact that executive pay of Global Fortune 500 companies has grown more quickly than the price of gold and 15 times more quickly than average wages is defended as the need to "keep quality." The analogy of world-class soccer teams is often rolled out—that the world's best managers and players need to be earning seven figures. Physical talent might be one thing—there is only one Usain Bolt, for example—but CEOs are scarcely as "unique" as sprinters. The premise that there are only a few thousand people on the planet with the talent needed to run the world's largest companies seems untenable. We don't use this logic for brain surgeons or lawyers, so why do we use it for CEOs?

This financial conundrum has prompted us to question whether business leaders should be allowed to negotiate packages which protect them financially if they fail and allow them even larger dividends if they succeed. As mentioned earlier, the whole issue of short-term incentives for investors and corporate leaders is being questioned. Shouldn't a CEO's pay be linked more directly to the long-term health of the company? After years of trying to encourage companies to appoint women Board members, the Norwegian Government has now mandated female representation. The German model of having workers directly represented on the supervisory Boards of leading German companies acts to make the whole process of remuneration more transparent and accountable, and also means that the salaries of German CEOs are less than half those of their US or UK peers. No one can seriously argue that German business is less competitive in the global marketplace as a result of its leaders being paid less. There might be an argument that there are too many white men on the Boards of most German companies, but then there are too many white men leading the trade unions, academic institutions, and NGOs too.

It is highly likely that the way a large company is governed will play an increasingly important role in its perceived legitimacy over years to come.

6. Shareholders, stakeholders, and rights-holders

It is pretty clear what shareholders are. They have shares.

"Stakeholder" is one of those CSR concepts that has crept in over the past 15 years—and seems to have a precise meaning, when in fact it does not. Literally, it is anyone who has a "stake" in a company. That, of course, could be anyone! In the case of some of the world's largest companies we all have a stake in their existence. Whether we buy their products of not, we cannot avoid their advertisements or sponsorship, nor how our children might come into contact with them when with friends. It is fashionable for large companies to have "stakeholder groups" or "stakeholder panels" to give them feedback on their performance and where they should be going. Unlike non-executive Board members, those on stakeholder panels rarely have any influence on the financial decisions of a company. Stakeholders are listened to, sometimes politely, but most companies are very bad at keeping any kind of feedback loop to those they have nominated as stakeholders. Sometimes, a company will send you their annual social report with the salutation "Dear Stakeholder." See, you were a stakeholder all along and didn't even know it!

Now "rights-holder" is beginning to creep into the lexicon as companies start to take human rights language seriously. It is a useful clarification, as not all shareholders or stakeholders have human rights and are therefore not "rights-holders" in this sense. A "rights-holder" is a person (not another company or some other institution) over which the company can have a social impact, be it positive or negative. Sometimes the "rights-holder" can be a community group, as in the case of indigenous peoples. In social contract terms, rights-holder is a much more meaningful concept that stakeholder, as it is the rights-holder that owns the social contract itself. Organizations are just direct or indirect manifestations of this.

Whilst individuals might (hopefully) be aware that they have human rights, they might not be aware that they are "rights-holders" in the eyes of a specific company. You might be siting peacefully at home whilst a supermarket chain is undertaking the early stages of an impact assessment for a possible development right beside your house. You will certainly come to hear about this at the formal planning stage, but you might not yet have been consulted by the company. However, you are still very much a rights-holder in the eyes of the company. You are someone upon whom the company's action could have an impact if it so decided. Workers, others working in supply chains, customers, community members, and individual investors can all be rights-holders, whilst the NGOs, investor groups, governments, and other companies which might claim to be stakeholders in the company are not themselves rights-holders.

In terms of legitimacy, it helps if a company is clear about who its rights-holders are and treats these relationships in ways that respect the human rights of those involved and the inherent dignity of each individual. Whilst rights-holders might be unaware of their potential relationship with a specific company, the company cannot choose who is a rights-holder and who is not, in much the same way a company cannot legitimately choose which human rights to respect and which to disregard. It is less legitimate for a company to continue using the stakeholder term unless it is clearly defined how someone becomes a stakeholder and which rights they in fact have. It is entirely illegitimate for a company to nominate its own "stakeholders" and those who are meant to represent them, listen politely to these self-appointed individuals once a year, and then proceed pretty much as they would have done anyway. It might lack legitimacy, but the practice remains prevalent.

7. Paying enough tax and in the right place

Much has been written about corporate tax avoidance over recent years, which I will not repeat here. It will be assumed that the reader is au fait with most of this. Whilst some of this tax avoidance has been legal, it is doubtful whether it will be perceived as being legitimate over the years ahead.

One facet of the tax justice debate that has perhaps not received enough attention is the way it privileges transnational companies. "Transfer pricing" plays a key role in minimizing tax. Companies recharge transactions internally, perhaps repeatedly for a single transaction, so that the transaction can be reported in a country with a low tax threshold or perhaps offering a "tax holiday" to new investors. Large companies do this all the time. It is a perfect storm in tax terms. A new market, wanting to make itself attractive to international investment, will allow companies a multi-year tax holiday. If internal pricing can legally allow that company to charge a significant amount of internal transactions to that new market, it can make the investment financially viable before the company has even sold a single product. This is anti-competitive behavior in the eyes of many, penalizing the majority of small and medium-sized companies that cannot engage in transfer pricing, as they do not operate across borders.

Whilst transfer pricing is a very complex area of international tax law and is (mostly) legal, it is less likely that it will be seen as being legitimate in the eyes of many.

What might make an activity legitimate?

1. Due diligence, mitigation, and prevention

Increasingly companies are expected to stop harms from occurring—to make prevention a key part of management. This is already apparent in health and safety policies and practices, and more recently in relation to international anti-corruption measures. Under an increasing number of jurisdictions, businesses are required to undertake due diligence to identify risks and take steps to reduce or prevent them. Businesses need to think not just in terms of risk to the business itself, but also in terms of risk to its employees, consumers, and any communities upon which it has an impact. Most recently, bodies such as the United Nations and OECD have also agreed that such due diligence requirements for business be extended to all their most significant human rights risks and impacts. I will explore these later.

Under the prevention paradigm, for a business to do nothing might cause it to lose legitimacy when dealing with risky products, markets, or suppliers. It might be seen as acting in a reckless or negligent way even if no harm ensues. The question, therefore, is how much due diligence should a business be expected to take? What is reasonable given that due diligence costs time and money (and it is not the primary profit-making purpose of any company, unless it is a law or accountancy firm)?

It might be that governments themselves will increasingly ask questions about the legitimacy of specific companies when making their own decisions about who to buy from (public procurement can represent 15–20 percent of an entire nation's GDP) and when to incentivize trade (via export credit guarantees or trade missions), when mediating complaints (under the OECD National Contact Point System) or even when buying shares (for example, the Norwegian Pension Fund—which invests the country's oil wealth for future generations—owns about 1 percent of all tradable shares worldwide). Governments are powerful economic actors. They do not need to threaten to revoke the legal license of a company in order to promote better business conduct, particularly in the case of publicly listed companies. It can be much harder when trying to influence cash-rich privately owned companies. This is partly a political license issue but it is also a legitimacy issue. CEOs do not like to be singled out for criticism by political leaders through public media in ways that have an impact on brand reputation and potentially their social license.

2. Adequate remedies

Remedies matter. Not just for the victims of corporate-related harms— and this, of course, is the primary purpose of legal and other forms of redress—but for the legitimacy of the company. Sometimes, in relatively well-regulated markets, consumer rights are relatively well protected and complaints are listened to, either by the industry itself or by an ombudsman or independent authority. In other cases, businesses can operate seemingly with impunity in terms of their impacts on workers and communities. The case of Trafigura is not widely known, but a minute or so on Google will show the reader that the company is "a leader in the global commodities market." Its website goes further:

> We source, store, blend and deliver oil and key raw materials to clients all over the world. We perform a simple task. We identify and act on imbalances between supply and demand. We achieve that by moving physical commodities from places where they're plentiful to where they're required.

This simple task can have complex consequences, as the Probo Koala case showed in 2006, when allegedly toxic waste which had traveled the oceans searching for a safe place to be off-loaded was disposed at open-air sites in Abijan in the Ivory Coast.

The rights and wrongs of this case are not the focus of this chapter, but they do challenge any easy understanding of what the legitimacy of a company really means. Trafigura is in rude health (posting record profits in 2013)—a leader in the industry, at least in terms of financial performance. Yet few members of the public will have heard of the company at all, even if many in the oil industry have. However, the case did cause quite a stir in British parliamentary circles, not least in the use of English libel law to issue injunctions to prevent the dissemination of allegations against the company by the BBC, the *Guardian* newspaper, and even (for a few hours, it seemed) parliament itself. UK libel law has since been reformed.

It is legitimate for a company to defend its interests using the law of the land. If the law is poorly framed, then the overzealous use of legal license might result in the curtailment of some political license until the law is reformed. But the Trafigura example might be held up as demonstrating the weakness of social license arguments. That the company sought to defend its legitimacy almost exclusively in legal terms, and with little impact on financial performance, it might be argued, defeats the argument for the need to invest time and energy in social license.

However, there is some indication that the lack of adequate remedies can adversely affect not just the perceived legitimacy of an organization, but also its social license over the longer term. Dow Chemicals is also a profitable company, but it acquired the legacy of the 1984 Bhopal chemical disaster when it bought Union Carbide in 2000. There have been a number of convictions under Indian law against the plant managers for causing death by negligence, resulting in two years' imprisonment and a fine of $2,000—the maximum allowed by Indian law. Other legal action continues. According to the Indian government, not only did 3,000 people die immediately after the incident, but at least another 15,000 have died since.[7] So although there have been legal remedies within India, these seem inadequate in comparison with the response to the 2010 BP Gulf of Mexico disaster. Damages paid after Bhopal relate to a few thousand dollars per death, whilst in the case of the Gulf of Mexico they will be equivalent to several billion (although not all for the victims' families). A fundamental legitimacy question remains unanswered: why is the life of an American citizen worth thousands of times more than that of someone in India when such disasters strike? Even if we accept the different economic contexts, the differential is unacceptable.

Even if inadequate remedies can affect feelings of legitimacy, do they necessarily affect the social license? Well, perhaps they do. During the 2012 London Olympics, the revelation that Dow Chemicals was one of the sponsors generated international adverse publicity—something the organizers had not predicted. This included threats to withdraw from the Games by the Indian Olympic Association. Whilst this had little adverse effect on share prices, it was commented at the time by a number of financial analysts that Dow's presence in India remains relatively small.[8] Union Carbide itself, owned by Dow Chemicals, is reported to be one-sixth the size it was prior to the 1984 disaster.[9] A proposed $100 million Dow Chemicals research and development center in Chakhan near Mumbai—hundreds of miles from Bhopal—was met with sit-ins by local villagers[10] and plans were dropped in 2010 due to "local agitation."[11] This does not mean that the activists were protesting over Bhopal—they may have their own local grievances—but clearly the Bhopal legacy (and the perceptions of the adequacy of the remedy given) casts a long shadow.

Causal relationships are very hard to prove, in particular when looking at issues as complex and subjective as the social license. However, it would be hard to deny that many question the legitimacy of the remedies following the Bhopal disaster (even other Indian business leaders have proposed the creation of an independent fund for cleaning up Bhopal).[12] And given these questions about legitimate remedies, the social license of the chemical industry in India is clearly still a pertinent issue 30 years after the initial disaster, as the 2012 Olympics sponsorship controversy shows. Whatever the rights or wrongs of whatever legal remedy is required, or the responsibilities of Dow Chemicals, the Indian government or whatever other actor, there seems to be a correlation between the adequacy of remedies, questions of legitimacy, and issues of ongoing social license.

I will return to the issue of remedies in relation to social license in Chapter 9 of this book.

3. Transparency and disclosure

Is transparency a good thing? This has become a debate of our time. At one end of the spectrum are what might be called transparency fundamentalists, who believe that the power imbalance between powerful organizations and the general public is so great that the ends justify the means in transparency terms. *Wikileaks* is perhaps the best-known example of this and—love him or hate him—Julian Assange has become an archetype of absolute transparency. Whilst still in the Ecuadorian Embassy in London at the start of 2014, he was given airtime by BBC Radio 4 in the "Thought for the Day" slot normally reserved for religious thinkers, and characterized the fight for knowledge and transparency in biblical terms, including the following:

> The invention of the printing press in Europe was opposed by the old powers of Europe as it spelled the end of their control of knowledge and therefore the end of their tenure as power brokers.... Knowledge has always flowed upwards to bishops and kings, not downward to serfs and slaves.... As our governments and corporations know more and more about us, we know less and less about them.... Today remember that it is good to seek to empower the powerless through knowledge and to drag the machinations of the powerful into the daylight. We must be unapologetic about the most basic of humanities: the desire to know.[13]

This is powerful stuff, and there is a strong linkage between power, knowledge, and transparency—see Chapter 8 of this book. On the question of legitimacy, how legitimate is it to dump large amounts of secret intelligence data into the public arena without controlling the adverse consequences of doing so? There is no consensus on this issue, although arguably there is greater support for the more targeted disclosures in relation to the US National Security Agency, revealing things that even US Presidents and German Chancellors were unaware of, than for the mass disclosure of *Wikileaks*.[14] What is certain, however, is that legitimacy cannot be sustained in any relationship if there is a heavy imbalance in terms of knowledge. In social license terms, an indigenous community negotiating with a mining company cannot be a legitimate process if the mining company is hiding from the community significant findings from its impact assessments.

The relationship between knowledge and the disclosure of that knowledge is a highly significant one when we consider both legitimacy and the social license. In Chapter 8, I will ask: when is transparency a precondition for maintaining the social license, and where might this not be the case? The premise I will test is that knowledge and the disclosure of that knowledge (so called "knowing and showing") underpin the legitimacy of so many aspects of both states and companies that increased transparency is indeed essential for social license to be engendered.

Concluding thoughts on legitimacy and social license

As stated at the start, social license for specific activities must not be seen as a way of short-cutting questions of organizational legitimacy—rather the opposite. Some element of legitimacy is required for social license to be established in the first place and will be required for its maintenance. Most of the examples in this chapter have related to business—and there seems to be a variety of ways in which legitimacy might be understood, many of which are relevant to the social license and are explored further later in this book. Although the chapter has taken examples from business, the legitimacy question is also relevant to governments and civil society organizations. Although governments will draw a lot of their legitimacy from their sovereign power and recognition amongst the community of states, this does not always mean that they will have de facto legitimacy in the eyes of all local communities—particularly in contexts of internal conflict, disputed territories, or calls for independence. The legitimacy of NGOs cannot be assumed either: whom do they represent and whose interests do they serve?

Each organization will need to find its own answers to questions of legitimacy. Essential to discussions on the social license is that these organizations have asked these questions and have their own answers to bring to the table when engaging with others in relation to specific activities. Other stakeholders are unlikely to agree with all these answers, but a robust exchange of perspectives on legitimacy is—as I hope to show—likely to create a stronger foundation for achieving and maintaining social license. Dodging the "L question" because it sounds too political, is above someone's pay scale, or might threaten an accumulation of tacit power is unlikely to allow an organization to progress far in the quest for a stronger social license in relation to a specific activity. One comforting fact (if it were needed) is that no organization of any type is immune from these questions and each should bring its own perceptions of its own legitimacy to a negotiating or partnership table.

5

Trust

Confidence in the relationship with those affected

"If you once forfeit the confidence of your fellow citizens, you can never regain their respect and esteem."

Abraham Lincoln (1854)[1]

Those who have written about the social license to operate identify *trust* as a foundational concept.[2] As the previous chapter has discussed, *legitimacy* as a concept relates to both the organization and the activity. A sufficient level of both is required for social license. Now, we turn our attention to *trust*—very much a relationship between the organization and the stakeholders and rights-holders concerned. The next chapter will look at *consent*, a concept that ties back the opinion of rights-holders to the activity in question. Whilst *trust* is very much a two-directional relationship, consent is not. It comes from the affected social groups in relation to the specific proposed activity.

"Trust" is not a small thing in business or governmental terms. "Trust" has been invoked as the cornerstone of many aspects of modern life, from consent-based policing in the UK to the legitimacy of the US Federal Reserve bank now that the world's currency of choice is no longer backed by gold bullion.

As with *legitimacy*, the danger is that we define *trust* in tautological terms such as "trust is earned through consistent trustworthy behavior over a long time." We all have an instinctive sense of what *trust* is, but definitions are nevertheless hard. The dictionary definition of trust is a "firm belief in the reliability, truth, ability or strength of someone or something." When it comes to friends or neighbors, we base our trust on our knowledge of their behavior towards us over months and years. It is based on reciprocity. Trust is established and maintained through active relationships. If one partner to the relationship acts in a way that undermines this trust repeatedly, then the trust each has in the other, and the relationship itself, will be under threat.

When it comes to trusting or not trusting organizations, public trust is notably fickle. Here the relationship is not necessarily between two people. More often it is between an individual, or a community, and a corporate entity of some kind. The relationship is often influenced by or mediated through a range of third parties, be they community leaders, politicians, the media, NGOs, or PR agencies. Given the challenges humans have in trusting organizations and not individual people, we should perhaps guard ourselves against having too high an expectation of what level of trust is actually possible.[3] Perhaps members of the public are prone to never fully trusting organizations, and perhaps some skepticism is a good thing.

Measuring trust in organizations

One interesting attempt to measure the public's trust in institutions is the annual "Trust Barometer" survey conducted by Edelman across 26 countries involving 31,000 respondents.[4] The findings give us a starting point. They suggest that less than one-fifth of the general public believes that business leaders and government officials will tell the truth when confronted by a difficult issue. Interestingly, there is a growing gap between the trust in organizations and the trust in the leaders of the same organizations.

"there is a growing gap between the trust in organizations and the trust in the leaders of the same organizations"

Example: The Edelman research specifies 16 attributes that build trust in relation to a business[5]

Engagement
1. Listens to customer needs and feedback
2. Treats employees well

3. Places customer needs ahead of profits
4. Communicates frequently and honestly on the state of its business

Integrity
5. Has ethical business practices
6. Takes responsible actions to address an issue or crisis
7. Has transparent and open business practices

Products and services
8. Offers high-quality products or services
9. Is an innovator of new products, services or ideas

Purpose
10. Works to protect or improve the environment
11. Addresses society's needs in its everyday business
12. Creates programs that positively impact the local community
13. Partners NGOs, governments, and third parties to address societal needs

Operations
14. Has highly regarded and widely admired top leadership
15. Ranks on a global list of top companies
16. Delivers consistent financial returns to investors.

So what do we think of this list? First, it is clearly focused on business and not on other types of organization. Second, if there is an element of "motherhood and apple pie" about the 16 attributes—they are apparently those which frame our perceptions of trust in relation to businesses. A similar study is conducted by Reader's Digest across 12 European countries each year and it also shows 16 criteria of trust.[6] The data seems to support the idea that it is better to be a well known brand than not to be known at all, and that it is the reliability, quality, and service provided by the product, as well as the retailer, which matters most to the customer. It is interesting that all these things seem to matter more to consumers than a low price. Social responsibility is creeping onto business agendas as a major factor just below pricing. Currently 59 percent of consumers state that they value social responsibility in relation to how much they trust a brand (it comes above transparency, strong image, local sourcing, and the reputation of senior managers). It is interesting to note that consumers in countries such as Poland and Finland seem to value social responsibility twice as much as do German shoppers when it comes to trusting a brand.

Such polls give us a starting point. They put a high premium on *transparency* (see Chapter 8 in this book). The importance of *transparency* is reinforced by other research in relation to the extractive industries. In Africa, for example, transparency on how revenues are collected and used is critical to establishing any basis of trust between communities, government, and business in relation to mining, oil, or gas exploitation.[7] However, many of the other Edelman and Reader's Digest attributes are what you might expect a well run business to do anyhow. If they were asked similar questions about their doctor, dentist, or garbage collector, it is likely that the respondents would cite similar issues of quality, reliability, and responsiveness of service. Who would not want those things?

The question of trust encompasses more than a citizen's ability to assess the trustworthiness of an organization. It seems that in terms of governments at least, a lack of knowledge is as much a trigger for trust as it is an obstacle to trust.[8] Citizens are blinkered in their own relationships with leaders. They might continue to trust a charismatic leader whom they know very little about and whose policies they have never scrutinized. So too it is with business. We can all think of brands which have maintained high levels of consumer trust despite allegations and evidence of negative social impacts in their operations. It seems that trust is indeed a fickle concept. However, it remains an important one all the same. It might actually be a good thing that the public do not trust organizations too much, even in good times. The evidence reviewed above suggests that during bad times, when a company or government behaves very badly or cannot manage a crisis, it is the trust in leaders that falls before the trust in the organizations themselves (which also remain generally distrusted, but not acutely so in most democracies).

The public and trust subjectivity

It is perhaps the case then that some brands are trusted too much. When I worked for The Body Shop International (which was a long time ago now) I was struck by just how little criticism we received and how global human rights and environmental NGOs were happy to partner us and not question the company's few internal inconsistencies—such as demanding that suppliers recognized the collective bargaining of workers whilst the company itself did not in its shops in some key markets. The Body Shop brand and the charismatic leadership of its founders acted as a "trust" shield or piggy bank, reminding us that trust is as much an emotive concept as it is a logical one.

Another source of trust data is the work of GlobeScan in key global markets.[9] What is extremely interesting is the divergence in the national respect ratings for specific business sectors in specific markets. The IT sector is perceived very well in Kenya and much more moderately in India: the ratings range from +55 in Kenya to –2 in India—both emerging economies.[10] Contrast this with the oil industry, for example:

> The oil industry is still feeling the reverberations of the 2010 Macondo spill in the Gulf of Mexico, which only recently led to a record-breaking fine imposed by the US government on its owner, BP. Despite this, the proportion of people saying there is insufficient government regulation has dropped in the US over the last two years, as it has also in Indonesia.[11]

Nevertheless, about half the surveyed population in countries such as China, the UK, and USA feel that there should be more government regulation of the industry, against only 35 percent in Nigeria and 17 percent in Indonesia. GlobeScan predicts that the industry will continue to face reputational challenges as it explores ever more remote locations in its search for oil and gas, with the associated huge environmental risks. But why should the Chinese be so much more concerned than the Indonesians about the oil and gas industry, or the Indians than the Kenyans about the IT sector? We need to introduce a new concept into the mix to help explain this—the concept of *salience*.

Some factors and some industries are much more meaningful to the general public than others, and this factor clearly varies as we move around the world. The BP oil spill in the Gulf of Mexico obviously has high negative salience in the USA and might continue to have for years to come. On the other hand, the IT industry in Kenya has huge positive salience. Sometimes the factors are indirect. The ever more urban Chinese are increasingly concerned about air and water pollution, and any industries perceived to being linked to pollution will suffer in reputation as a result. As to why the IT sector might have negative salience in India, I will leave it to others to explain.

It is clear that the salience of particular industries shifts in the public consciousness. The IT industry, which can still do so little wrong in Kenya, would not receive a similar rating in a country such as Sweden, where a leading mobile phone operator has been mired in allegations of corruption and abuse of human rights across a number of challenging markets. GlobeScan also predicts a shift:

> ... respect has been slipping in many markets and cost remains a major concern for many consumers, raising the prospect of a "digital divide." Privacy is also an increasing concern, following widely publicized missteps by some of the sector's major players like Google and Facebook in the way they use consumer data—and only likely to become more salient as the value of consumer profile data continues to grow.[12]

A problem for companies has been that the salience of issues in the minds of consumers has tended to be at least five years behind the actual performance of companies. When stopped in the street, some members of the public will associate with certain brands child labor scandals that were material in the 1990s but from which the brand has since moved on, now actually having some of the best management systems in place to minimize the risk of further abuses. However, the company is rarely rewarded for this in the public's mind, or in the mind of important opinion-formers, such as politicians or the media.

Theory one: Low levels of trust don't actually matter too much because the public is itself complicit or apathetic

There are two readings of this ongoing distrust of sectors and issues and the lack of any full restitution of trust in companies that have moved on to better practices. First, it could be argued that the public is right not to fully forgive and to point to the death of 1,100 people in the Rana Plaza tragedy in Bangladesh in 2013 as evidence that nothing has really changed. The fundamental premise of sourcing apparel and footwear from the very cheapest countries in the world has not changed. So why should any consumer trust that the due diligence undertaken by any specific company will matter a dime when the system values the dignity and value of human labor so poorly? This is a truth that will be picked up again and again in this book—that trust can never be fully achieved by any organization (which is perhaps a good thing) and that even moderate levels of trust cannot be recovered if the sector itself is communicating incoherent or even contradictory messages to the wider world.

In a nutshell, the message from the apparel sector has been something like: "don't expect us to stop sourcing the cheapest labor on the planet where social and environmental risks are very high, though, of course, we will do our best to minimize the risks within our supply chains." The implications of this are: (1) Don't be surprised when disasters such as Rana Plaza happen. However, it's about wider issues of poor governance and corruption. We just bring highly valued jobs to a very poor country, and (2) by the way, you the consumer, continue to buy our clothing and you seem to like the low prices. So, you are in many ways complicit.

As shown earlier, trust is not a one-way relationship. It is not just about the consumer trusting the company; it is also about the company's relationship with the consumer. Most consumers know, in their hearts, that whilst they continue to reward companies for providing them with $10–15 jeans and $3–5 T-shirts, they are complicit in the status quo. In a sense, consumers do not fully trust themselves either. Therefore, some business sectors might never achieve high levels of trust because both company and consumer share some complicity in maintaining the status quo. Whilst the business sector might not be highly trusted, consumers are unlikely to punish individual companies for their mistakes.

"trust is not a one-way relationship"

Theory two: The public need better information to know which organizations to trust

The second, competing, theory is that the 5–10-year time lag between the realities of social and environmental performance and how the public perceives companies has been due to corporate responsibility being a very new field. The theory holds that more accurate perceptions of a company's non-financial performance will come with better knowledge (you might recall the quote by Julian Assange in the last chapter). There has been a big push to greater transparency across global supply chains, from nutritional information on supermarket products and austere warnings on tobacco products, to transparency on oil and gas revenues to help prevent the "resource curse."[13] The assumption is that greater transparency is, on balance, a good thing, and that greater publicly held knowledge will result in greater accountability.

One of the biggest push factors towards better information and knowledge has been the investment community, or at least the more socially responsible fringes of it. The effort here has been to promote "environmental, social, and governance" (ESG) factors as keys to assessing the performance of companies. A number of indices have also been created, such as FTSE 4 Good Index and the Dow Jones Sustainability Index, to incentivize companies to actually report on these issues—and, one would hope, perform better as a result, if the reports are indeed an accurate representation of what the companies actually do and the decisions they make. It is very much the "tail wagging the dog," but as the dog has been largely under-interested, the tail has indeed been a good place to start.

The broad-based alliance of socially responsible investors that adhere to the "Principles on Responsible Investment" claim to have $35 trillion of assets under management.[14] This sounds like a lot, and it is, but it is still a drop in the global investment ocean. The largest SRI by far is the Norwegian State Pension Fund, which owns about 1 percent of globally available public shares and is increasing its own ESG requirements of the companies it invests in. Such investors have been able to bring the leadership of companies such as Walmart to the ESG table and the vast majority of Global Fortune 500 companies now have publicly-stated social and environmental policies and most report on aspects of their ESG performance.

It is important to remember that the vast majority of global investment, and certainly global trade, goes on day in and day out with no reference whatsoever to ESG criteria. But if current trends continue there is good reason to suppose that at some point more systemic market change will occur. The lobbying positions taken by Al Gore, with his Generation Investments fund, Richard Branson and Paul Polman, through the B-Team initiative, and others will gradually receive mainstream attention. Whilst there is no evidence that good ESG management necessarily causes good financial returns, there is increasing evidence of a strong correlation. Other related efforts, such as ending quarterly reporting to investors and linking executive pay only to short-term performance, are also gathering some momentum. At a minimum, ESG management is a good indicator of company management overall and therefore should be of material interest to all investors. If concepts such as the subject of this book are going to be mainstream to business and other institutions as argued in these pages, then the investment community will be a key driver for the social license over the years and decades ahead. In this way, it can be argued that, for investors at least, greater knowledge of company performance does deliver greater levels of trust.

Has this led to increasing levels of public trust? There is no evidence of this yet, and again we might speculate as to why. As the "trust" academic experts remind us, there is no evidence for increased levels of knowledge being correlated with increased levels of public trust in any kind of institution. In fact, greater knowledge might result in less trust. If we take tobacco products, for example, public trust has fallen only as smoking has itself becoming socially less acceptable in many countries—not because of alleged fabrications of scientific evidence by some tobacco companies in the 1950s and 1960s. My reading of the Edelman, Readers Digest, and GlobeScan research is that the trust of institutions, if not necessarily their leaders, does seem to settle around a mid-range of 30–60 percent for most organizations and, where most companies can only hope to remain. Increased knowledge of harm will not necessarily tip a company below the threshold of tolerance. It seems that knowledge has to be accompanied by a number of other factors.

Different ways of trusting and implications for social license

The trust that specialists have in institutions—such as the investors in a company, the media, or NGOs—seems to correlate to some extent to knowledge of the actual performance of the institution. Trust, as a component of social license, seems to be more objectively framed in such relationships. They are perhaps closer to the way that trust works in interpersonal relationships.

When we consider the way in which the wider public views institutions, then things seem much more complex. To some extent, public attitudes are framed by the way that specialists view these institutions—in particular those in the media or politicians. In terms of the two theories above, it is likely that there is some truth in both of them—good knowledge is important for public decision-making. But there is also a range of irrational and emotional aspects to the relationship: feelings that the actions of an individual make little difference in reality, complicity with the status quo, concerns about price, or just general apathy. A lot depends on what issues are most salient for the public in specific countries, and this might be as much to do with general societal, economic, or cultural factors as with the actual performance of the organization.

Whilst the public is more likely to trust the leader of an organization than the organization itself, provided that the leader is known to them, this can work in reverse if the leader falls from grace. Levels of organizational trust seem to stay within a range of 30–60 percent, except in extreme cases. However, if a leader has become known by the public and disliked, governments and companies will tend to pin the blame on them when facing reputational challenges, even if the responsibility is more collectively held.

The subset of the public that includes consumers or community members impacted by an organization locally might therefore behave in a number of ways depending on how well they know the organization in question. If the organization wants to be more objectively judged, then it needs to empower consumers or communities to behave more like informed specialists than members of the general public.

In social license terms this is the central conclusion of this chapter on trust. For trust to be an enabler to social license in a way that can be managed, organizations should foster informed relationships rather than generic ones. Therefore, the organization needs to invest in strategies that empower stakeholders and rights-holders to be informed partners able to absorb and process knowledge and information about performance. Strong community leaders, the media, NGOs, and other specialists will have a very significant part to play. The result will be much more political relationships, but there is still a need for a baseline of knowledge if the right kind of trust dynamic is established. The other option is for organizations to treat stakeholders as if they were random members of the public and to accept mediocre levels of trust in perpetuity—driven mainly by external societal factors. For social license to be a meaningful concept the former approach is required.

chapter 6

Consent

Granting necessary permission for an activity

"Companies come to us wanting to consult with us about their operations. They often want to know how long it will take our community to respond. We tell them that sometimes it will take one night, sometimes one day, sometimes it might be a week, a month or even years. It depends on the question they ask."

Indigenous leader, El Estor, Izabal Guatemala (2013)[1]

There was once a mining company that was desperate to open a mine deep within the Australian outback. The challenge for the company was the fact that the mine would sit upon the land of indigenous peoples. Under Australian law, the company needed to gain the consent of the local community before any mining could start. Every month, the company's anthropologist went to talk to the village elders. One old lady sat there in silence during every visit with her eyes closed, letting the men of the village voice their fears and concerns. The anthropologist was concerned by the silence of the woman. She wanted all the elders to speak. She wanted to consult fully. After two years of visits, the community was still withholding its consent. After one awkwardly long silence, the anthropologist was surprised to see that the woman had opened her eyes. The woman fixed the anthropologist in a long stare and said in her broad Aussie accent: "What part of 'no' don't you understand?"[2]

Whilst the previous chapters on *legitimacy* and *trust* related to organizations and the relationship between them, *consent* moves us on to the specific activity—the realm of social license itself. Analyst is working to achieve social license without the *consent* of a local community would initially seem to be an oxymoron. Consent seems to be a large part of what social license is about. The relationship between consent and social license will be explored more deeply in this chapter, starting with examples relating to indigenous peoples—which have already been extensively analysed—and then taking in some wider examples. *Consent* will be seen to be a more complex concept than on first inspection and one where the different interests involved in social license do not always align.

"consent seems to be a large part of what social license is about"

Consent and indigenous peoples

There are currently 30,000 active mines in the world. Although the rate of growth of mining slackened during the 2007–12 financial crisis, the longer-term trend within the global mining sector is clearly one of expansion. Map 6.1 below shows how mining correlates geographically with the remaining presence of so-called indigenous peoples around the world. Put simply, the geological profiles that are richest in the minerals and metals that modern society needs are the often those unsuitable for farming—and so hence are where indigenous communities are still extant. This means that every mining company operating in a number of global locations needs to consider the rights of indigenous peoples if they are to secure social, or even legal, license.

For many years, indeed, centuries, indigenous people have been at the rotten end of a bad deal. Ninety percent of the indigenous population of the Americas was wiped out by Europeans and their diseases between the 15th and 19th centuries, and other indigenous peoples have been marginalized in their own countries—in Australia, New Zealand, and many parts of Asia. In Africa, the very concept of indigeneity remains a contentious one. Most Africans rightly believe they are indigenous to their own continent (but did we not all originate from that continent at one point in time?). This hides the reality that majority ethnicities practicing farming have displaced migratory hunter-gatherer communities over recent centuries.

MAP 6.1 Global density of mining activity

Source: Intierra Resource Intelligence (October 2011). Reproduced by kind permission.

So, if recognized indigenous peoples represent such a small percentage of the global population, why does a chapter on "consultation and consent" start with a focus on them? The answer lies in the efforts of the past 30 to 40 years to give these communities some protection against further exploitation and encroachment. Indigenous peoples exist largely outside of the mainstream political system and therefore need specific protection under international law—in this way "free, prior, and informed consent" can be seen as an important procedural right.

The UN Special Rapporteur on Indigenous Peoples, James Anaya, has helpfully clarified the interpretation of *consent*.[3] He writes that states need to

> consult and cooperate in good faith with indigenous peoples through their own representative institutions in order to obtain their free, prior and informed consent before adopting and implementing legislative or administrative measures that may affect them … a significant, direct impact on indigenous peoples' lives establishes a strong presumption that the proposed measure should not go forward without indigenous peoples' consent. In certain contexts, that presumption may harden into a prohibition of the measure or project in the absence of indigenous consent.

In 2007 the United Nations General Assembly recognized this wider concept of "Free, Prior and Informed" consent in a Declaration supported by 144 governments.[4]

More specifically, the components of Free, Prior, and Informed Consent (FPIC) are defined as:

* *Free* implies "no coercion, intimidation or manipulation";
* *Prior* implies that "consent is obtained in advance of the activity associated with the decision being made, and includes the time necessary to allow indigenous peoples to undertake their own decision-making processes";
* *Informed* implies that "indigenous peoples have been provided [with] all information relating to the activity and that that information is objective, accurate and presented in a manner and form understandable [by] indigenous peoples";
* *Consent* implies "that indigenous peoples have agreed to the activity that is the subject of the relevant decision, which may also be subject to conditions."[5]

Whilst the concept of FPIC is internationally recognized, it is in Latin America that it has been applied most clearly. The International Labour Organization Treaty on Indigenous People (Convention 169), which recognizes FPIC in relation to community relocation,[6] has been ratified by most Latin American countries but by very few countries outside of that region. In fact, they can be listed here: Central African Republic, the Netherlands, Norway, Nepal, and Fiji. Organizations such as First Peoples Worldwide point out that there are still too many governments that deny the existence of indigenous peoples outright and therefore any right of consent.[7]

In a 2007 decision the Inter-American Court of Human Rights invoked the need for consent for any type of project that has a "significant impact" on an indigenous community.[8] Consent, then, matters a lot; it can be seen as a strong procedural safeguard for marginalized communities in relation to all their other human rights. The direction of travel in international law is clear: governments should not allow a project to proceed when the consent of an indigenous community is absent, even when national law allows them to do so.

The global mining industry has also now engaged directly on the consent issue. In 2013 the International Council on Mining and Metals (ICMM), representing 22 of the world's largest mining companies, itself took a public position on FPIC and indigenous peoples, stating that its members should:

> Work to obtain the consent of indigenous communities for new projects (and changes to existing projects) on lands traditionally owned by or under customary use of Indigenous Peoples that are likely to have significant adverse impacts on Indigenous Peoples.[9]

Note the words "work to obtain." The Council is also clear that its members should not see the absence of consent as an automatic "veto":

> These processes should neither confer veto rights to individuals or sub-groups nor require unanimous support from potentially impacted Indigenous Peoples (unless legally mandated).

There is also an emphasis on "good faith" negotiations, that is, that they should be on an equitable basis. "Consent processes," in the view of the ICMM, should focus on reaching agreement so that projects might proceed.

This is very much a positivist understanding of consent, that processes should be premised by a willingness from both the mining company and the indigenous community to find a mutually acceptable path forward.

From this perspective, the absence of consent, whilst highly undesirable, does not require an ICMM member company to abandon a project. However, in social license terms, consent is a prerequisite and companies should expect to face indigenous community opposition when attempting to proceed without consent. Amy Lehr (2014) puts it clearly in social license terms:

> The most obvious challenge for a company that seeks FPIC is that it might fail to obtain consent and be unable to move forward. A company's inability to obtain FPIC is a strong indicator that it does not possess a social license to operate, so proceeding in such instances could lead to operational shut-downs and adverse media attention, regardless of whether [the] company has a policy [of] requiring consultation or consent.[10]

Thirty years ago it was easier for an extractive company to enforce its will, particularly in Latin America, as there was likely to be a military dictatorship in the capital willing to deploy troops and guns to enforce the will of the state. Democratic governments are less likely to open fire when communities block construction or access roads. National and international civil society organizations can use modern media to bring the attention of the world to the plight of a specific community. Occasionally they can also take legal action.

In Peru and Ecuador there are many examples of social license being lost due to the absence of consent. Sometimes, however, things can be done well. One example of achieving social license based on consent that I have seen relates to a mining project in Chile that was defended not just by the company but also the indigenous community in question. Amongst the factors cited as contributing to its success (at least to date) are:

- The fact that the national government participated in the consultation process from the start and that it is a government that has ratified ILO Convention 169;
- Central government set the broad context for consultation and consent, with the involvement of NGOs and regional government in addition to the community organizations;

- The process was not rushed and a clear timeline was set. Consultation lasted for 18 months and the rules of the game were made clear from the start as well as the purpose of the consultation;
- Social development issues were also identified early on and were delegated to three commissions focusing on (1) water, (2) environment, and (3) social investment. A lot of the discussion then happened at a very concrete and practical level, with working groups composed of the different rights-holders and stakeholders involved.

From the company perspective, the approach should be one that embodies the basic components of human rights due diligence, as already set out in this book. In relation to recording the consent itself, Amy Lehr advises companies to do the following:

> Consent should be memorialized, ideally in a written format. Consent could also be captured through video recording if the community is mostly illiterate. The agreement should state:
>
> - The nature of the project;
> - Any benefits that will accrue to the community;
> - Mitigation steps the company will take to address risks;
> - The stage or stages of the project that the agreement includes;
> - Project milestones at which the company would need to obtain consent for additional activities or other planned steps; and
> - Monitoring mechanisms or any other means through which the community and company will continue to engage.
>
> Even after a community expresses consent to a project, a company should continue to engage with the community in order to maintain its social license to operate. A company may also need to later obtain consent for unforeseen and substantial changes to the project. For these two reasons, some companies set up mechanisms that enable ongoing interactions with communities that keep both sides informed, and allow concerns to be addressed.[11]

So, "free, prior, and informed consent" can be meaningful when it facilitates an agreed process between indigenous peoples and other organizations, in particular companies and governments. But to have any meaning, social license requires consent. Any company advancing a project without the consent of a community, through its recognized and representative decision-making processes, does not have social license—I would see this as a necessary truth in definitional terms as well as a practical one.

But achieving consent can be easier said than done. Traditional decision-making powers in a community might not be very representative; powerful individual interests might dominate and so the need to agree on representative processes is fundamental even if consent does not mean consensus any more than it means an automatic veto. Consent is best understood as an ongoing process which maintains both the social license and the legitimacy of any project. When indigenous communities are highly marginalized, this poses some practical dilemmas. For consent to be a meaningful and lasting concept—one that might result in a social license— indigenous communities need to be equal partners in all negotiations.

"consent is best understood as an ongoing process which maintains both the social license and the legitimacy of any project"

This presents challenges for communities which are themselves highly marginalized. Should they accept offers of legal assistance paid for by the company? Which local or international NGOs should they trust to support them? Recognizing the asymmetry of power that exists between many companies and indigenous communities is one thing, but doing something about it in a way that maintains the legitimacy of the relationship is another. There are a number of mining projects that have strong indigenous involvement (for example in Australia) or ownership (in parts of Canada and on tribal lands in the USA). There are mining projects where deeper issues of power and ownership have been addressed, resulting in power sharing and real benefits for the community concerned (I will look at "benefits" and "power" as social license issues in their own right in Chapters 7 and 8, respectively).

Consent beyond indigenous peoples

The right of "free, prior, and informed consent" is a fundamental one, and there is much discussion as to whether vulnerable communities should enjoy the same procedural rights as indigenous peoples. Some, such as the international NGO Oxfam, have called for the concept of FPIC, or at least some aspects of it, to be widened beyond indigenous peoples to all communities worldwide:

> Community consent is also emerging more broadly as a principle of best practice for sustainable development. We [Oxfam] believe all project-affected communities must be able to participate in effective decision-making and negotiation in processes that affect them—and that when they say "no" to a project this should be accounted for.[12]

Interestingly, Oxfam has also linked widening of the consent principle to an attack on the traditional interpretations of social license as used by many oil, gas, and mining companies:

> Although social license suggests a positive relationship between a company and its neighbours, corporations when pressed are rarely willing to equate social license with community consent—that is, corporations aren't willing to withdraw operations in places when communities are opposed to their presence. The distinction between social license and consent is critical because accepting community consent as a basic operating standard sets a high bar. If a community's actual consent is required before operations begin, companies must treat the community as more of a partner in project development.[13]

I agree with the spirit of the above statement. There are countless other marginalized communities around the world that are not classified as indigenous and that have very few legal protections for their rights if a government or business decides to take their land away or exploit it in some way. But there is, at present, no international consensus that community rights should trump the will of the majority nor agreement on the threshold of vulnerability which would trigger such a safeguard were it possible to achieve. Hopefully greater international agreement about which other types of vulnerable group (such as the extremely poor, slum dwellers, the internally displaced, or the historically disadvantaged) require a similar procedural entitlement to FPIC might be achieved. But trying to build out from the significant but limited success that FPIC has achieved for indigenous peoples is a sign of a failure of legal systems in many parts of the world to adequately protect the vulnerable and most disempowered.

Moving beyond this, I see a wider problem. Many communities, not just the most marginalized ones, will demand the right of consent to activities that impact on their lives. But the need to have local consent for every development need in a country would have very serious consequences. We might not like to have a power station near our house, but if citizens vote for a government that plans to develop such energy sources, then some of them are going to have to put the needs of the majority before their own. Many middle-class areas oppose the building of socially affordable housing in their midst, fearful of how this might impact on house prices, local schools, and the crime rate. Should governments only pander to middle-class concerns? Wind farms illustrate the point even better. A majority of people in most countries support cleaner energy, but still, when it comes to building wind turbines, there is often local opposition. Hence the term Nimby (not in my back yard).

So policymakers have two societal tendencies to balance: the justifiable need to protect the rights of vulnerable communities when confronted with powerful economic and political interests, on the one hand, with that of *Nimbyism*. In both cases the community might still claim a right of consent, even if they are not vulnerable or traditional in the same way. Both can lead to the undermining of social license. However, one is based on a legitimate need for protection, whilst the other needs to be challenged by expressing the rights of the majority and the consent already given to national governments to override local consent when it is clearly in the national interest. Not easy! It is particularly difficult when governments do not represent the interests of the whole of society, but rather an elite. Who decides when a country needs another golf course, mega-sporting stadium, or high-speed railway?

It is amazing how poorly many governments handle the issue of consultation and consent. For example, the recent controversy (2013) over fracking (mining "shale gas" or "coal-bed methane") in the United Kingdom has been characterized by emotiveness, a lack of impartial information, and government ministers running for the hills instead of engaging in debate. Rather than leading a national debate about the pros and cons of fracking, the government granted export licenses and the exploration companies offered local communities financial "incentives" for their consent. Unsurprisingly, the social license was challenged: yes, partly by some local residents, but mainly by national environmental interest groups. If the social license for fracking in the UK is lost, governments will only have themselves to blame. We can add to the list the handling of the genetically modified crops debate in the 1990s or that relating to nuclear energy in the UK. Governments in democracies are not incentivized to make decisions in the long-term interests of a country. To do so they have to take political risks. Whatever the rights or wrongs of fracking, it is hard to believe that the debate has been managed with the social license in mind.

It is an unfortunate fact that many politicians and business leaders perceive the public as risk-averse, and that any national debate will scare populations and lead to bad decisions, tying the hands of policy-makers for decades to come. There is some truth to the matter, if policy were made in accordance with opinion polls, it is likely that the UK would have the death penalty, zero immigration, be isolated from Europe, and have a completely dysfunctional foreign policy. When countries or regions allow the population to suggest and then vote on issues of national policy, they can end up with very strange decisions—such as the suspending of gay marriage in California or the banning of minarets in Switzerland. Governments know this and have created structures that can override the consent of the people—such as the Supreme Court, which reinstated gay marriage in California, and the European Court of Human Rights, which is likely to require the Swiss state to end religious discrimination against Muslims. However, at the end of the day, to achieve and maintain freedom takes a lot of hard and ongoing work, and entails many uncomfortable realities for a liberal elite, as the Thomas Paine quote earlier in this book indicated.

Thus, when we move beyond the most vulnerable, "community consent" should not be seen in isolation from the interests of the wider society—in other words "national consent." It has to be balanced against wider public interests. It is true that sometimes national elites will abuse this argument, and trample local communities in the pursuit of personal, elite, or business interests rather than those of the majority. Hence the need for strong transparency and accountability mechanisms, which I will discuss in Chapter 8. To give all local communities an automatic right of veto to development would further segregate communities from each other within nations and not always represent the interests of the marginalized.

In this way, indigenous peoples are an important exception. For them, FPIC is fundamentally an issue of self-determination. The nation state was imposed upon them in most cases and so consent should be regarded as a procedural human right. When any local community is disempowered and vulnerable, the principles of free, prior, and informed consultation with the objective of achieving consent matters greatly. So do other safeguards within societies to protect the marginalized and poor. To suggest that FPIC is equivalent to an automatic right of veto, or that it should be a substantive right for everyone and not just indigenous peoples, risks undermining the particular protections indigenous peoples have fought so hard to achieve.

I accept that in many parts of the world, particularly the global South, marginalized communities which are not deemed to be indigenous are in desperate need of greater protection against issues such as land grabbing, illegal eviction, and exploitation. I agree with the spirit of Oxfam's position on extending FPIC to all, but reluctantly feel that in practice a more thoughtful approach is needed. If social license is set up outside of the concept of consent, then, indeed, the social license to operate concept can be dismissed. However, I argue the reverse: that consent (despite its many complexities) is intrinsic to the social license concept and it is meaningless to talk about social license without it.

The problem with "tacit consent"

So the need to achieve the consent of local or national populations for every decision is not an absolute for legal or political license (with the exception of indigenous peoples), but it is a fundamental concept for social license. Whilst social license might be understood purely in terms of consent in the short term, it needs to be balanced with concepts such as legitimacy (discussed in Chapter 4) and trust in leadership and decision-making processes (Chapter 5). Leadership structures that really understand the long-term interests of a country are essential for its long-term wellbeing. These structures need to be democratically accountable. The decisions themselves should not always be subject to consent. Rather, consent is required to the fact that every country needs leaders who can sometimes make unpopular decisions. It is the processes themselves that need to be accountable, not the decisions made. This is the underpinning concept of most democracies, eloquently stated in 1776 in the US Declaration of Independence:

> We hold these truths to be self-evident, that all men are created equal, that they are endowed by their Creator with certain unalienable Rights, that among these are Life, Liberty and the pursuit of Happiness.—That to secure these rights, Governments are instituted among Men, deriving their just powers from the consent of the governed.[14]

The "consent of the governed" has become the mantra for all those who believe in democracy, since the words were first spoken at the first congress of the (13) United States of America on 4 July 1776. Whilst the 1948 Universal Declaration of Human Rights does not specify democracy in particular, it does clearly state that the authority of government is derived from the "will of the people."[15] Consent, then, matters a lot.

The trouble with consent as understood in the democratic tradition is that most of us do not overtly consent to everything that happens in our lives. We live in societies where most of the laws that govern us were written long before we were born, and where officials (elected, hopefully) make many of the decisions on our behalf, without even consulting us. Therefore, we live in a world where it is "tacit consent" that more accurately describes how we are governed. If we do not vote against a political party or actively protest against an establishment that defies the will of the people, then we are tacitly consenting to their governance over us or on our behalf (whichever might be more accurate). Some writers, such as Chomsky, remind us that what might look like freely given consent can be manipulated by the media and other powerful actors in society. This is why the notion of consent that is both "freely given" and "informed" is important—terms that will be examined more closely shortly.

Those born and living in relatively functional democracies might not worry too much about consent in their day-to-day lives. The concept will come into focus when they make major life choices, such as whom to marry, where to live, or when their neighbor wants to build a big extension right up to the boundary wall. They will then be asked for their consent or will request it from others. This process might well involve consultation, discussion with family members, the advice of expert third parties, and so on. In some societies individuals are able to give their consent independently. In others they will want to consult family members, and in others it is the community as a whole that needs to give its consent.

Although a government has been elected, and has the consent of the people (and also the ruling monarch, president, religious leader, cabal of generals, and whatever special arrangements a particular state might have), it might decide that it needs to achieve more overt consent in relation to a big national decision, especially if the latter has constitutional implications. This book is written as the UK looks towards the possibility of two referenda inviting the consent of some or all of its people. In the first place, on the issue of Scottish independence in 2014, only the Scots are being asked for their consent. On the issue of the UK's future within the European Union, only those with British nationality will be asked. Let's leave aside the issue of what will happen if the Scots are no longer British or those living in Northern Ireland who do not identify with British nationality. Other governments have felt the need to ask their peoples for similar consent for issues such as German reunification, the Treaty of Lisbon, independence from a colonial power, a peace treaty ending a civil war, whether to join the United Nations, and so on. In some countries, constitutions allow the will of the people to be expressed directly through ballots or in the form of "propositions", which can defy the will of a government. A proposition in California denied gay people the right to marry until it was overturned by the US Supreme Court in 2013. Similarly, a ballot in Switzerland led to the prohibition of the building of any more minarets within the country, an act of religious intolerance that is at the time of writing (2014) before the European Court of Human Rights.

So there are clearly limitations on how consent can operate in practice. If asked shortly after a horrific murder or terrorist bombing, the people of most countries would vote to reinstate the death penalty, even though more and more nations are either abolishing its use or increasingly limiting its application. For this reason, the protection of fundamental rights is often enshrined in a country's constitution or bill of rights, requiring a two-thirds or greater parliamentary majority to be overturned. States bind themselves still further by signing international treaties, making it still harder for the "will of the people" to prevail on every issue. The truth is, and no elected politician will ever say this whilst sober, the people do not always know or understand what is in their own or their nation's best interests. Capital punishment might be a good example of this. It should not be an issue of consent, at least not one of short-term popular consent.

However, we are on much more tricky ground when we deny people the right of civil disobedience. Over a million people marched through the streets of London to try to prevent the invasion of Iraq—an invasion at that time based on "facts" about chemical and nuclear capabilities that turned out to be false. There was no referendum at the time to find out whether the largest act of civil protest in modern British history represented the majority view, but opinion polls suggested that it did. Despite this likely absence of popular consent, did the Prime Minister Tony Blair then have the right to declare war and invade another sovereign nation? Well, arguably, yes. There was a vote in the British parliament that he won. The British people had already given their tacit consent by electing these MPs. But to deny the British people a direct voice in a decision with such long-term foreign policy implications does not seem to balance with the fact that the British people are now being directly consulted on two sovereignty issues.

The reality is that few governments will make issues of foreign policy issues of consent. There are a number of reasons for this, including the complexity of diplomatic relations, the need to bluff an enemy government, the natural distaste most societies have for war, and the time lag this would create in times of fast-moving emergency. Government might also draw some comfort from the fact that foreign policy seems to remain its most popular domain in terms of the electorate's trust (as discussed in Chapter 5). In terms of the core issue of the social license, governments (and this includes democracies) can enforce their will through the law, the arrest of protestors, control of the media, and the selective use of information. Over the longer term, however, it can be argued that governments—and in particular their leaders—will lose the social license for their activities when they operate without overt consent.

The benefits of active participation and consent

Sherry Arnstein observed the importance of local consent when looking at town planning across the USA during the 1960s.[16] Her eight-rung ladder of citizen participation has been used by sociologists and political scientists since to show the benefits of involving citizens meaningfully in decision making. There are many who sit in positions of power who have not read her work. The way that the public discussion on the benefits and risks of genetically modified organisms (GMOs) was handled is a textbook example. Regardless of the facts, in the absence of a meaningful process of consultation with the public in Europe, most governments banned even research into the issue for a whole generation. However, companies such as Monsanto were caught largely off guard by the deficit in consent. If we wind forward to 2013, it is arguable that the British government has made similar mistakes over the handling of the fracking issue in the UK—ceding the argument to the activists so that exploration companies are seeing local consent erode before their eyes (and with it threats to the social license for their activities).[17] However, there are examples of the UK government leading an open dialog and achieving consent, whether this relates to the smoking ban or the fight against HIV/AIDS and a more widespread change of attitudes to sexual orientation within British society.

In my opinion, it is not that governments don't understand the importance of consultation and striving for consent—rather they fear that the general public are not good at making decisions about risk. It is classically the case that members of the public will become very concerned about horsemeat in hamburgers (with no proven health risks) but will routinely speed in urban areas (with very real health risks). Policymakers fear that any discussion about risky technologies such as fracking, nuclear energy, or GMOs will lead to emotive discussions where the evidence will be lost and that risk, even of very unlikely events, will dominate public feeling.

However, if governments can do it for HIV and AIDS, and hundreds of years of homophobia, then nothing should be impossible. Perhaps at the end of the day, consultation and consent-focused processes are more an issue of political will.

Consent and the internet

The consent to be governed is not the only contemporary example of the how the concept of consent is relevant to communities and the wider population. One-third of the world's population, 2.4 billion people, are now internet users and each will be consenting to use some form of internet service provider,[18] most with little knowledge about what they are consenting to in terms of data privacy. For the vast majority of internet users this has yet to become a problem of any kind. The upside of information and communication technology is immense, and it has brought with it greater freedom of expression, access to information, and the opportunity to enjoy many other human rights. Given this important heritage, it almost seems petulant to characterize the internet as a risk as well as an opportunity but it is important we do so given the stakes involved.

It was the case of the journalist Shi Tao in China in 2004 that started to alert civil society to the risks. Shi Tao had summarized a verbal censorship instruction his newspaper had received in an email to US-based activists, and Chinese security authorities had intercepted the email. When clicking to open his account, Shi Tao had undoubtedly infringed an online tickbox consent form that did not allow the transfer of state communications. Yahoo argued that they were required under Chinese law to hand over Shi Tao's personal details when requested to do so by the authorities, obviously without Shi Tao's consent. Shi Tao was charged with leaking state secrets on 11 March 2005 and sentenced to 10 years' imprisonment. As Rebecca MacKinnon reflects in her book *Consent of the Networked*, "legally Yahoo were off the hook, but ethically they weren't."[19]

What companies such as Yahoo, Google, and Microsoft have done over recent years to minimize the risk of similar human rights abuses will be the subject of part of the final section of this book, which discusses possible future trends. Whilst the Shi Tao incident is unknown to the vast majority of internet users, some of the privacy challenges facing companies such as Facebook are increasingly discussed and the Edward Snowden revelations of 2013 show that consent and privacy are pressing issues for mobile operators as well as internet service providers, and that the dilemmas relate to many security services, not just the Chinese. The social license issue relating to the governance of the internet is a fundamental one: can some governments or businesses be trusted to legitimately navigate these tensions between consent, personal privacy, and national security, or are non-state actors essential in such decision-making wherever in the world it is? As MacKinnon puts it: will the social contract between the internet and the internet user over the years to come be framed in Hobbesian or Lockean terms?[20]

The essential point is that user and public trust is the fundamental social license issue for internet and mobile operators in the 21st century—as fundamental to them as the apparently more tangible/palpable trust issues that mining and oil companies have (until recently) faced. But there are in fact useful parallels. A mining company needs consent to mine the land, an activity that will make profit for the company. Online service providers whose business model relies on users sharing personal information, such as Facebook, need consent from users to collect and store their data, which is shared with advertisers, and therefore makes Facebook a profit. The difference with the internet is that consent can be withdrawn from companies if the user deletes their account and, in theory, the information held therein, or chooses another service provider.

Some final thoughts on consent and social license

For the first time in human history, many of our choices are recorded within the digital realm and will be accessible for decades, if not centuries to come. To what extent will our children or our children's children need to account for the choices we make and will their privacy be secure given the consent we give, often tacitly, today? Consent is fundamental to the social license not only now but also for years to come. In the non-digital realm, this chapter has looked at the issue of consent in relation to major projects or decisions made by governments or companies. On the one hand, free, prior, and informed consent is an essential procedural right for indigenous peoples in relation to activities that impact upon them. On the other hand, the consent of the more general population, whilst also an important principle, is more complex, and there are times when local consent needs to be overruled in the national interest. The next part of this book will look at structures that can help develop social license for activities. Consent, like legitimacy, is a core concept that needs to be embodied in these structures.

Final reflections on the three core concepts: legitimacy, consent, and trust

This part of the book has set out the reasons why legitimacy, consent, and trust should be regarded as core to the social license, as preconditions for it. Having adequate levels of legitimacy, consent, and trust do not automatically create social license, but without all three social license cannot be sustained. Legitimacy relates to the organization(s) in question, trust to the relationships between them and stakeholders and rights-holders, whilst consent relates to specific activities.

Social license might serve to strengthen legitimacy, but more fundamentally some level of legitimacy must come from external or historic factors. For an organization to claim legitimacy purely based on social license is not just tautological, it is also highly likely to be seen as illegitimate to at least one of the main stakeholder groups. Rather, organizations need to assess their own legitimacy and bring such claims to any negotiations with stakeholders relating to specific activities (projects, policy development, practices, product development, marketing, etc.) for which social license is required. Stakeholders can then interrogate the basis of each other's legitimacy and assess whether there is a mutual basis for advancing the relationship. Trying to avoid questions of organizational legitimacy is unlikely to advance social license over the medium to longer term, as implicit concerns are likely to surface.

Consent is required for many types of social license to be created and over the longer term it is better for this consent to be explicit rather than tacit. Consent is most robust when it is freely given before a project, policy, or practice is initiated, and is based on objective information. The consultation processes that embody such an understanding of consent need to be strongly protected as a procedural right for indigenous peoples but also, in different modalities, for other vulnerable and marginalized groups in society. The absence of consent does not always represent an absolute veto, but it does require organizations—and in particular governments—to explain why overruling some element of consent reflects majority interests. However, the absence of consent is likely to destroy any basis for local social license for a specific project, just as it will weaken the social license of governments and other organizations that routinely defy the will of a population.

Finally, as argued in this chapter, trust is another prerequisite for social license. The evidence suggests that legitimate organizations are better served by developing "informed" relationships whenever possible, as these are more likely to be based on objective than subjective assessments of an organization's performance. This implies that organizations need to take steps to develop such relationships and to empower stakeholders to be as informed as possible—a theme to be explored in the remainder of this book.

Part 3

Building and Losing Conditions for the Social License

7

Benefits

The delivery of sufficiently positive outcomes for all concerned

"It is hard to measure the absence of a human rights abuse."
Salil Tripathi (2014)[1]

I have already commented, earlier in this book, that I do not believe the social license can be managed directly or claimed by an organization itself in relation to a specific activity. It is more a state of affairs that reflects a balanced relationship with the pre-existing social contract in a society. Part 2 of this book has looked at some of the foundations that need to be in place for social license to emerge—factors that an organization does have some degree of control over. However, the leverage is often limited by many other societal, political, and other factors. Even if these foundations are in place, social license is not guaranteed. This part of the book moves on to look at a range of other factors over which an organization has more control. Again, these do not infer any mechanistic relationship between what an organization does and its social license, but solid performance on the issues contained in these chapters must, in my view at least, increase the chances of a balance with the social contract and therefore of a strong social license emerging.

Social contract theory reminds us that both "contract-based" and "justice-based" considerations need to be part of any approach toward understanding the social contract. The same then is true of the social license. These contract-based considerations are explored in this chapter on *benefits*. However, just as important are justice-based considerations. They might not relate to the material nature of the relationship—the products, services, or information provided—but more to the national and international standards and norms that condition the way society is governed. Justice-based considerations are the focus for the last two chapters of this part: *addressing power imbalances* and the need for *prevention* and *remedies* for potential and actual victims.

This divide between contract-based and justice-based considerations is not absolute. They are, of course, closely interrelated. The sweep of the next three chapters should capture this relationship. As mentioned, the factors examined in Part 3—more than those in Part 2—are directly manageable by the organization itself. They do not automatically ensure the social license. In not managing these issues an organization is not managing its risks and impacts, and therefore is like the group of blind men touching the elephant in the famous Jain and Hindu fable.[2] Each man touches a different part of the elephant (trunk, tusks, legs, tail, etc.) and then builds his own very different idea of what the beast must look like. An argument ensues and it is only when a sighted man walks by and talks to them that the full picture of the elephant is understood.

If an organization has the social license under such conditions, it is more by luck than good judgment—making assumptions based on a partial understanding. The organization concerned can never claim that it is taking reasonable steps to manage what could reasonably be expected of it.

Benefits for whom?

And so to this, the first of the chapters: *benefits*. All activities that are not purely natural phenomena happen for a reason. Organizations embark on activities because that is what organizations do—they do stuff. These activities might be well thought through and underpinned by strategies or business plans. They might be highly opportunistic, reacting to events, or they might be shambolic, poorly planned, or almost random. But there will always be a reason somewhere. So when asking why an organization does something, we must first ask whose interests the activity is in. What are the benefits and for whom?

Large organizations and, implicitly, smaller ones, often state in their constitutions or mission statements the purposes for which they exist. For governments it should be to perform a sovereign duty on behalf of the whole population (if only it were always true); for a business to return a profit to shareholders (if it is publicly listed), its owners (if privately owned), its staff (if a partnership), or its customers (if a cooperative). Some businesses are explicitly "not for profit" or charities and these organizations will often be exempt from corporation or business tax for this reason. The term non-governmental organization (NGO) is poorly defined but tends to equate with this "not-for-profit" category of organization—as do trade unions, religious organizations, independent schools, and so on. Few organizations, of any category, will embark on an activity which does not benefit them in some way or another. However, for an activity to gain social license, the benefits have to be felt more widely—in particular in the social groups affected by the said activity.

"for an activity to gain social license, the benefits have to be felt by the social groups affected"

Social benefits of the social license

The nature of the social contract has varied and so too have its associated benefits. In China, for example, the "old social contract" that existed between the 1950s and the 1970s was based on "firm-floor living standards in return for political quiescence ... a contract with normative appeals for sacrifice on behalf of the nation and the building of socialism."[3] The new social contract of the last 20 years has been rather based on remunerative appeal, with higher personal incomes. This is seen as bringing great economic and social benefits to the nation, but also new challenges, such as growing economic division and corruption.[4]

Can collective visions for society be developed in truly democratic ways, or are they—almost by definition—the preoccupation of non-democratic governments trying to maintain social cohesion?

In many European countries a vision of what constitutes social harmony is unstated at the national level, where the future is often envisaged in terms of returning to some of the great achievements of the past, or of protecting national identity. Arguably, the European Union does have a relatively clear and overt vision of Europe's future—focused on 2020:

> The Europe 2020 strategy is about delivering growth that is: smart through more effective investments in education, research and innovation; sustainable, thanks to a decisive move towards a low-carbon economy; and inclusive, with a strong emphasis on job creation and poverty reduction. The strategy is focused on five ambitious goals in the areas of employment, innovation, education, poverty reduction and climate/energy.[5]

Such social and economic visions are just that: visions. Whilst I have already defined social license as relating to specific activities, outputs and outcomes need to be aligned so we can see the need for social license to align with any social vision commonly held by stakeholders.

Most human rights NGOs will rightly focus on the protection agenda—preventing rights being violated as well as holding to account all of those who violate them. However, there is much less clarity on what a society, business, or community that respects human rights looks like. The Universal Declaration of Human Rights, first signed in 1948, gives us a clue in the start of its preamble:

> Recognition of the inherent dignity and of the equal and inalienable rights of all members of the human family is the foundation of freedom, justice and peace in the world.[6]

The experts of the Commission on Human Rights, who worked between 1946 and 1948 to produce the Universal Declaration, drew on many consultations and research to try to ensure that the moral vision of the newly established United Nations would stand the test of time.

The stated social visions of the United Nations as a whole, and the European Union and China more specifically, seem, at face value, to be well aligned with each other. Who would not want these things? What they all share is a sense of benefits—benefits in the interest of society as a whole. Where they might differ is in the unspoken detail—the methods governments and others should use to achieve the visions.

Some would argue that the concept of human rights, upon which much of the authority of the United Nations is built in social contract terms, is a "poor bedfellow" with concepts such as "harmony," much discussed in contemporary China: "does not individual striving to protect one's human rights smack of disharmony?"[7] US professor Stephen Angle argues that there is no intrinsic contradiction between the Confucian analects and modern understandings of human rights (and therefore, I would also argue, between social contract theory and the social license concept). Angle's central argument is that harmony does not mean control. In social contract terms, it does not mean that the *Leviathan* should oppress dissent only to maintain stability. He argues that a correct interpretation of harmony includes an understanding of the dynamic nature of society, with increasing participation by everyone and a balance of competing interests. Such a view, whilst not the reality in China or anywhere else at present, is an interpretation of harmony that is compatible with, and indeed reliant upon, human rights.

One of the weaknesses of the focus on human rights is that it provides no view of the "end state" of any community or society, except in very simplistic terms. If we are working for a world in which no human rights will ever be abused, then this is not a utopian vision of the world. Rather it is a hell of stagnation and inert humanity that resembles nothing of a Shakespearean observation of the human condition.

Human rights, like Angle's view of harmony, are also about a constant balancing act between competing interests and sometimes competing human rights. For example, the right to freedom of expression is limited by protections against hate speech and inciting violence (protecting the right to life itself), whilst the right to information is constrained by justifiable issues of privacy. Whilst the right to privacy is often seen in terms of protecting the rich and famous from press intrusion (the poor have no privacy!), over the years ahead it will be about us all—or at least all those with a Facebook or Google account.

Therefore, harmony and human rights share some common characteristics, and whilst harmony needs human rights to be legitimate, so too does human rights need some concept of harmony in order to better realize the balance between the two required in society. It is therefore surprising and disappointing that so many in government and in civil society have seen these two concepts as polar opposites. They clearly are not, on closer inspection, but the idea of social harmony has been misused by governments as much as the term human rights.

Economic benefits and the social license

Economic benefits matter. Whether it be fracking in England, oil in Scotland or Kenya, uranium mining in Australia, or even an agreement to build a new shopping center in a town, the first issue most politicians will address is the economic benefits for the community in question. All too often the economics are simplistically stated. The value of a hundred new supermarket jobs is rarely set against the opportunity cost faced by local small shop owners, entrepreneurs, or SMEs. It is no coincidence that one of the greatest grievances of local communities in relation to mega-sporting events, such as the Soccer World Cup in South Africa or Brazil, is the fact that local merchants are often unable to sell products within a wide radius of sporting arenas. It must not be forgotten that the much-vaunted (but somewhat crushed) hope of the "Arab Spring" started in a marketplace in Tunis. If an activity is commercial, or has a commercial dimension, then economic benefits will be expected and organizations must work hard to both set and meet expectations appropriately.

Take the example of Kenya. The organization I currently direct has worked for a few years, with local partners, to ensure that human rights impacts are considered right at the beginning of oil and gas exploration in East Africa—years before oil starts flowing. In a nutshell, the aim is to help East Africa to avoid the "resource curse" that has plagued other parts of the world, and particularly West and Central Africa. One of the target constituencies is the often small "exploration companies" that few people have ever heard of, often registered in Canada, the UK, or Australia (in the case of Asia). These exploration companies are set up purely with the purpose of finding reserves of onshore oil or gas, and then most often to sell it on to one of the major oil companies for full production. With only a 5 percent chance of finding exploitable oil in most cases, costs are kept to a minimum. Why should these companies use time and money on community consultation, on considerations such as the social license?

The focus of our work is building the case for such companies to care about human rights risks and impacts. This means building the capacity and awareness of governments (home and host), civil society, and the companies themselves. It also means being very clear about economic benefits. This puts on the table immediately the issue of revenue-sharing—not least because oil has been discovered around Lake Turkana, a region of Kenya that has only a loose affinity to the nation's capital in Nairobi.

One of the dilemmas of oil and gas exploration is the extent to which a country's hopes of revenue are raised by just having geologists visit their land, when the chances of any revenue being generated are only 5 percent for a whole district, and therefore much less for a specific village. This means informing communities not just about the potential economic benefits but also about the likelihood that these benefits will go to some other community elsewhere in Kenya, and not to them. A tricky dynamic, and one which has not been very well managed anywhere in the world, as the UK fracking non-debate demonstrates. However, it raises the issue that revenue-sharing with local communities is not just an issue of local concern. The percentage that goes to the national government (and not the community that sits beside the find) is, in part, the economic benefit for every other community in the country. It suggests immediately that the numbers and ratios involved in revenue-sharing need to be agreed before anything is found anywhere, and that discussions on economic benefit are held at the national level—not just locally.

Some interesting work is starting to emerge about the true nature of economic benefits and the way these impact on society more widely. Work conducted between Unilever and Oxfam in 2005 deserves particular mention here, as it is still relatively unusual for there to be collaboration between an international corporation and an international NGO in investigating the issue of social and economic benefits in Indonesia. It should be noted that Oxfam operated completely impartially and without accepting any financial contribution from Unilever. From the perspective of Unilever, the research shows that the company's 75-year history in the country has produced clear economic benefits: 5,000 direct jobs having been generated to date, with another 300,000 involved in the wider value chain selling Unilever products. Two-thirds of the economic value of Unilever's activities in Indonesia lies outside of Unilever Indonesia. One important finding was that the economic benefits to poor people were not automatic and required positive intervention:

> However, from our research it also became clearer that participation in value chains alone does not guarantee improvements in the living conditions of poor people. For value chains to work for poor people, there needs to be other social institutions and resources in place, such as credit and saving schemes, marketing associations and insurance schemes.[8]

Oxfam and Unilever collaborated again in 2011 to look at the impact of Unilever's supply chain in Vietnam.[9] This time benefits were measured against international standards. Wages were found to be significantly above local minimum wage levels and the international poverty line, but below regional living wage standards. In terms of related social benefits, whilst management were able to bargain collectively for their terms and conditions, blue-collar workers were not. Oxfam America has also collaborated with Coca-Cola and SAB Miller and has pushed the "people-centered" and participatory methodology of such collaboration still further.[10]

So economic benefits are difficult to assess. When they are looked at in isolation, at the national level, it can be maintained very credibly that exposure to international markets—including the supply chains of large companies—generally confers greater economic benefits than would alternative jobs in the domestic sector. This was true even of the 1,100 workers killed in the 2013 Rana Plaza factory collapse in Bangladesh: the women earned much more than they would have done if they had stayed in their villages. But the social license will not allow benefits to be considered in such a ring-fenced way. The wages workers earn in global supply chains are in part compared to the value of the products themselves, as well as ideas not just of minimum or poverty wages, but what might constitute a living wage. Achieving a living wage requires empowerment of workers and economic benefits require social benefits to be fully realized.

If good practice means that economic benefits cannot come at the expense of social benefits—and that both need to seen within an increasingly international and not just national context—then companies need to do more than just ensure compliance with their own standards. If they operate in countries where poor collective bargaining is the norm (such as Vietnam) or where workplace sexual exploitation is known to happen (such as Kenya), then heightened due diligence is required. Bad things should not just be acted upon if they are found. High theoretical risk is in itself is a good enough reason to take strong proactive steps. I am aware that Unilever knows this. I cite them here because they are a company willing to take the first steps, as their work in Indonesia and Vietnam shows. Most companies are not willing to even contemplate the question, and the consumer remains ignorant of and/or complacent about such things. So proactive companies get little economic benefit themselves.

Inequality in benefits

The work of the philosopher John Rawls reminds us that sometimes a level of inequality is needed to arrive at public economics that benefit the whole of society. In terms of benefits, this means that the economic or social benefits of an activity might not be equally shared amongst a community or a population. As discussed, there might be good reasons why a local population takes a greater share from the benefits of a mining, oil, or gas operation—even though the minerals under the ground are, in most countries, owned by the government on behalf of all the people of the nation. All societies, even North Korea, pay their brain surgeons more than their road sweepers, and this is largely to incentivize people to strive for such goals and endure the many years of training and study.

As Rawls also reminds us, the social contract can only prosper if the positions in society that receive the higher rewards are open to all—a meritocracy in other words. Arguably then, in all societies that are run by unaccountable elites, or where the division between the richest and poorest is so vast that it cannot be justified in social contract terms, social licenses for specific activities will eventually wither. There are countless examples in history of governments pushing inequality too far and losing their social license. The large-scale public opposition in the UK to Margaret Thatcher's "poll tax" is but one example, echoing protests against unjust taxes and levies from down the ages. The American War of Independence was sparked by the Boston Tea Party, in defiance of British taxes on its North American colony. The "Tea Party" term was revived more recently by the more radical fringes of the Republican Party in an attempt to devolve powers from Washington DC to the people of America. Just for the record, I was part of the poll tax protests in the UK, but have no affinity with the Tea Party movement in the USA. However, the point is the same: social license can be challenged if perceived inequality in benefits is not explained, understood, or accepted.

"social license can be challenged if perceived inequality in benefits is not explained, understood, or accepted"

One of the challenges for Brazil, Russia, India, China, and South Africa, as well as many of the key emerging economies, is the growing disparity between the very richest and the poor. Whilst in relative terms there are fewer people living in abject poverty than there were a generation ago, there is greater economic inequality in most societies around the world. Even the former socialist President Lula of Brazil sent his children to private school.

If there is one overarching "take-away" from this chapter, it is that all organizations do well to constantly explain the rationale for social and economic benefits, and why any inequalities persist. Defending extraordinarily high CEO pay and benefits purely in terms of the competition that exists between Global Fortune 500 companies for a small group of superstars—the only ones gifted and experienced enough to do so—will not cut it. It is premised on the idea that there is no higher motivation than personal economic benefit and that this is why CEOs get out of bed in the morning, not for the challenge, a sense of duty, or commitments made to colleagues.

It is not coincidental that the issue of politicians' pay is even much more controversial than that of CEOs. Government, as the creation of the social contract, is accountable to the people and therefore economic benefits have to be explained in a way that most people understand. Should a politician earn more or less than a brain surgeon, the same as a senior civil servant, and so on? The social contract requires a transparent logic. When politicians vote to increase their income by stealth, fearing the public would never understand a pay increase, this can fundamentally threaten their social license (as the MP expenses scandal in the UK has shown).

Because business is perceived to sit largely outside of the social contract, anger about CEO pay is not quite on the same scale—or at least it has not been historically. More recent protests, such as the Wall Street Reform or the 1 percent protests, indicate that something is changing—that CEO pay is being understood as erosive to the social contract. Two of the businesses to come out of the recent financial crisis in the UK better than most are the John Lewis Partnership and the Nationwide building society, which share their economic benefits with their workers (in the case of the former) and their customers (in the case of the latter). It is also the case that the CEOs of both these businesses are paid well, but not at the same rates as those of competitor supermarkets and banks.

It is quite possible that as concepts such as the social license are better understood and accepted in years to come, CEO pay will need to be justified in social terms more than just industry competition terms (more akin to the way that the pay of politicians is defended). The same will be true of company profits, bonuses, revenue-sharing agreements, and so on. Such organizations would do well to start thinking through how they might engage the public in these discussions. And yes, businesses need to think much more carefully about the true social benefits of their existence.

8

Tackling imbalances of power

Knowledge, participation, transparency, and accountability

"A prince therefore who desires to maintain himself must learn not always to be good."

Niccolò Machiavelli (1515)

"A body of men holding themselves accountable to nobody ought not to be trusted by anybody."

Thomas Paine (1791)[1]

I don't think I have ever attended a CSR conference that has dealt with the issue of corporate, civil society, or governmental power. Perhaps I simply missed the invitation email. However, no serious discussion on social license can be advanced without an evaluation of what imbalances of power between different state and non-state actors mean in social contract terms. Some organizations are clearly more powerful than others—either in real terms or in perceptual terms, or both. This chapter can make only a very superficial excursion into the subject but will address the issue of how imbalances of power might be tackled through interventions such as the acquisition of knowledge, participation, transparency, and accountability.

Power

There is so much in Shakespeare's work and countless modern political writers that speaks about the issue of power that there is little new to be said here, other than the context in which I am saying it. I would like to make a number of initial observations about the multi-stakeholder world that is the focus of this book.

First, it is quite possible for those in powerful organizations to underestimate their power and resulting impacts, and overestimate the power of others. I have sat around many tables over the years where the NGO representative (feeling underpaid and overworked) will look at the multinational company representative (feeling marginalized in their own organization with no clear lines of authority) as the powerful actor, who will in turn look to the government representative (feeling out on a limb), who will look back at the NGO (who might be able to change their minister's mind). Actual power and perceived power are very different things, but perceived power can have a powerful impact on how others behave.

At the local level it is often easier to agree where the real power lies. The power gradient between a multinational company and a local community is often so steep that it warps a process, preventing it from being "free and informed." As Aung San Suu Kyi stated in 1991:

> It is not power that corrupts but fear. Fear of losing power corrupts those who wield it and fear of the scourge of power corrupts those who are subject to it.[2]

It is often the fear of power, or perceived power, that can generate tacit consent to activities: the fear of a powerful company and its links to an oppressive government, the fear of violent men who run the village, the fear of the unknown or losing a way of life, a livelihood, a culture, an identity.

Even those who represent powerful organizations do not always feel powerful. Unlike Machiavelli's Prince they do not have clear lines of authority. They might be trapped in a matrix management system, which means that decisions are made collectively or not at all. Powerful organizations will often have competing power structures within them. During my own time working for a company, it was very much a question of the "monarchy" (the founders and head franchisees around the world) competing with the "republic" (the new CEO and formal management structure) for control of the company. Of course, a country director of a major company can have considerable amounts of autonomy, and if it is a private company even more so. So be sure when you sit opposite them at a table you know which of the two ("monarchy" or "republic") you are dealing with and, if you are the business representative, be sure you know this about yourself too.

There will be hierarchies between government ministries that determine where the real power sits on these issues. Often it is the Ministry of Foreign Affairs that signs up to global standards on issues such as fighting corruption, environmental protection, and human rights; other government ministries are sometimes less enthusiastic. It might be much more oppositional when it comes to implementation. A few years ago I witnessed the government of a leading emerging economy supporting the business and human rights framework within the United Nations (led by its Foreign Ministry) but opposing the same framework within the World Bank Group (because it was led by its Ministry of Finance). Sometimes, the distance between two government ministries in a capital city can be very great.

Power, therefore, matters a lot. What is to be done about it in terms of the social license? To be aware of its existence and to not take assertions, promises, or claims at face value until deeper investigations of the organization in question have been carried out. This is why this chapter also looks at knowledge and participation. Understanding power dynamics needs to be part of a due diligence process any organization undertakes before taking major decisions. This does not necessarily mean lines of lawyers or political consultancies. At a community level it might be done by thorough consultation, questioning, and discussion. Some people are born with "political DNA," whilst others are born blindly naïve to such things. Make sure that it's the politically savvy who undertake the due diligence.

Knowledge

The quote from Julian Assange in Chapter 4 was included with provocative intent. He is surely right that knowledge is a very significant part of power. This is what the "informed" in "free, prior, and informed consent" means.

When it comes to the social license, what is the kind of knowledge that matters? There are different types of knowledge that are relevant:

- *Knowledge about organizations*: What the organization is, its owner-ship and governance? In whose interests does it act? Can it be trusted? And so on.
- *Knowledge about actual and potential activities*: What are the risks and opportunities posed by specific intended activities? What are the impacts of actual and potential activities? What mitigations and preven-tative measures have been undertaken?
- *Knowledge about intentions*: Perhaps the most Machiavellian of the three types of relevant knowledge. What are the institutional and personal motivations at play? What are the longer-term implications of an organization's actions? What is true and what is not?

For consent to be informed, the organization in question needs to have some understanding of all three types of knowledge. Trust will also depend on some level of knowledge and will be undermined by revelations that information has been withheld or distorted. However, information is not knowledge in itself: information needs to be processed and interpreted adequately for it to become knowledge. Therefore, the disclosure and transparency of information do not necessarily empower those who most need it. The internet today is littered with information, much of it produced by organizations and some of it very relevant to those trying to understand a specific organization or its activities better. But it might remain inaccessible because it cannot be found within the sea of information out there, or it is in the wrong language, or a particular community does not have access to the internet. And, of course, there is much very important information that is not publicly available.

So whilst knowledge is clearly an important element of legal license to operate, there are two competing thresholds. The first, from criminal law, usually makes intention (which can include knowledge) an important element in the definition of the crime and so makes it crucial for establishing criminal responsibility. Therefore, in some cases, a defendant may claim in their defense that they did not have knowledge of the risk. The second, from some forms of tort, civil, or administrative law, makes knowledge an expectation in seeking to prevent harm from occurring—fundamentally it becomes irrelevant whether the defendant knew or did not know; they should have known. If they took mitigating or preventative steps in light of the knowledge of the risk then this may be an important part of their defense to a claim.

The consequences of these two approaches can be seen in the corporate world. There is a clear incentive in contexts where criminal liability is a risk to ensure that the controlling hand of a company is shielded from decisions that bring the company owner into a position of having knowledge of serious harms that might be caused to others by the company or its subsidiaries. The parent company–subsidiary relationship is often complex, but is used to separate parent companies from the liability of their subsidiaries. There may be little incentive for a company's headquarters to acquire lots of knowledge about high-risk decisions by its subsidiaries, the impacts of which might not be or only very partially be in the control of the parent company. But where the actions of a subsidiary have in some form been directed by the parent company, it may be possible to "pierce the corporate veil" and hold the parent liable.

When social or environmental factors become accepted norms—often through legislation but not exclusively so—the logic for the company flips. It is better to have had the knowledge, or certainly to demonstrate that you had due diligence and preventative measures in place to both acquire it and act on it—certainly to a level that might be "reasonably expected." This is where companies are positioned, in most parts of the world, on issues of health and safety. Workplace fatalities are unacceptable in most geographies and are only tolerated when mine owners, for example, can honestly report that all reasonable preventative measures have been taken.

Onto this conflicted stage walks the social license to operate. As with other issues, the legal confusion on the issue of knowledge both reflects and conditions the non-legal societal norm. In some cases businesses have been very secretive about the fact that you have the knowledge, thinking it best not to have knowledge of social risk at all, or at least to shield senior officers from the paper or email trail. We see it everywhere, from the International Criminal Court, to enquiries into media empires, to high-profile corruption cases in any number of countries, to the use of products or weapons to kill innocent people. Did the organization know about the harm that might have occurred? Should they have known? Did they take appropriate preventative measures?

Participation

In the Brong-Ahafo region of Ghana, 180 miles from Accra, sits one of the largest open-cast gold mines in the world. Exploiting the ore required the resettlement of over 400 households, many of which relied solely on farming for their livelihood. An additional 1,300 households were economically displaced, many of which also relied solely on farming for their livelihood. The rights and wrongs of gold mining will not be argued here: we can all—if we wish—now buy gold products that are certified as ethically traded. What is interesting in this case is how the mining company in question, Newmont Gold, approached the issue of community participation, conscious as it was of the power imbalances that existed between the company and the community and within the community itself.[3]

The question of traditional status is critical to any social license in rural Ghana. Paramount chiefs exert control over sub-chiefs and lesser chiefs in the following areas: custody of stool lands (lands belonging to a traditional community which are allocated by the Traditional Leader); leadership and control of inhabitants living on stool lands; maintenance of the cultural heritage; mobilization of the population for development efforts; and local arbitration and settlement of disputes. At face value, there is a clear and legitimate power structure for the company to engage with.

The only problem is that all of the above are men, and men of a certain age. Does this matter? What right does a company have to impose values of gender and age equality on any community, particularly as such discrimination exists in many societies? The principle of participation is a universal one—embedded in several United Nations Human Rights Conventions as well as in the constitutions of many countries, not least Ghana, which has one of Africa's most proactive national human rights institutions. The fact that full participation is a principle that has never been achieved anywhere in the world does not mean that it is any less applicable in rural Ghana. Some far-sighted individuals working for the company within that context at that time understood this.

Representative committees of women and young people were created by the company. These in turn were represented on the Resettlement

Negotiation Committee, which oversaw all the key resettlement and compensation decisions. Traditional owners were encouraged to cede some power to others in the community when the new communities were established. At the time the company stated:

> Resettlement rarely if ever results in complete satisfaction for all those affected. Some people may have already been vulnerable due to family circumstances or predisposed to vulnerability due to conditions existing prior to the project. This can be exacerbated by resettlement, with certain groups, such as the elderly and the sick, being more at risk than others.[4]

Therefore, the "Guards of the Earth and the Vulnerable" was created by local communities, funded by Newmont, to assist those most in need during the transition. In 2006, 459 households were placed in the Food Basket Assistance program, a number which had dropped by 307 three years later. When reflecting on the lessons learned, the local managers stated:

> Community engagement, relationships, and the negotiation processes are very important and require the investment of significant time and energy from the very start. These processes must also take into account local culture and must be established to determine what the correct forms and magnitude of compensation might be to ensure that the company respects the community members' rights to earn a decent living and to acceptable housing. Whilst the exact process and outcomes may vary according to [the] context, it is critical that companies give appropriate time and energy to community engagement and that they do not underestimate the value of these processes.[5]

A cry from the heart, one feels, and one directed at the mining sector itself, as much as to any other stakeholder. It is perhaps disappointing, therefore, that many in the extractive sectors still see human rights issues as "above-ground risks," at best, not as an integral part of the legitimacy of the company itself. Any of us working on the softer issues, "the world savers," as Tony Hayward put it, are used to being tolerated at mainstream industry conferences, to speaking on the final panel of the day, as people start leaving for the airport, long after the government minister has left. Companies routinely underestimate the value of these processes. Such processes are not costed into exploration contracts or included in acquisitions processes. They do not constitute costs that investors are willing to see on balance sheets. Participation has yet to be valued by those who put a price on things.

But the social license certainly requires participation. For example, most parents decide not to join parents' governing bodies of the schools to which they send their children. However, they would be upset if no parent undertook this duty and it was purely in the hands of local government or some private interests. We expect our hospitals to have some oversight mechanism, the police to be subject to a complaints body, and so on.

In this book I claim that social license is a modern manifestation of the social contract. If this is the case, social license must be aligned with what can be described as consent-based and justice-based components of social contract theory. Power, knowledge, and participation are grouped together here, partly because they are interrelated but also because they are intrinsic to building consent-based aspects of the social license.

"social license must be aligned with what can be described as consent-based and justice-based components of social contract theory"

If a mining company wishes to empower a local indigenous community association in a consultation process with the aim of achieving free, prior, and informed consent, is it legitimate for it to fund the community group in question, to pay for their lawyer or training, or for their own project impact assessment? I can feel various readers wanting to shout out "Of course," whilst others are shouting "Of course not!" Yet these are questions we have to deal with if we want social license to be a meaningful concept. Here are a number of observations from my own experience:

- Transparency in regard to where funding comes from is essential. To be trusted, organizations must be transparent about their funding sources, even if it conceals the size of individual donations. If an organization does nothing else, it should fund transparency and I leave others to draw their own conclusions thereon.
- Funding from an organization that is part of a specific activity to which the recipient organization is also party changes the dynamic

of the relationship. For example, if a business pays an NGO to write a report about its performance or even wider issues facing the sector, the resulting report can be very valuable. However, do not expect it to be perceived as impartial. It is essentially consultancy, even if the resulting report is made public.

- Funding from governments can permit greater impartiality (depending, of course, on which government is giving the funding and how it is given), but donors still have their own agendas and targets to reach. There can be great benefit in creating "donor groups" where several governments join together and can, to some extent, hold each to account as well as balance various competing interests. It is a truism that significant donations from large, powerful governments, which are not balanced by similar donations from elsewhere, will raise concerns about some level of co-option.

- Businesses funding community-based organizations directly in relation to a consultation process can create a tricky situation, and it is hard to see how impartiality can be preserved. Is the consent granted really freely given? If it is, will it be perceived as such? Is it not possible for a levy to be applied to the whole sector, which can fund lawyers and NGOs more impartially? Can national governments and other donors also contribute to this?

Transparency

You can have transparency without truth, but you can't have truth without transparency. Historians, journalists, and police detectives all need to get their facts from somewhere. It might be argued that this is disclosure and not transparency. Dragging information from a witness is the same thing as proactively sharing facts in reports, press releases, or on your website. However, there is no such thing as absolute transparency; nor does transparency in itself always enable the truth to be known. As discussed in the previous chapter, information is a prerequisite of knowledge but is not the same thing. Similarly, although transparency can enable greater accountability, it will not achieve it on its own, and at the end of the day, for building social license it is accountability that matters more than openness.

What is needed is *meaningful transparency*. Just placing information in the public domain does not necessarily, in itself, reveal the truth—as discussed earlier in this book. The Extractive Industries Transparency Initiative put a report relating to oil revenues into the public domain, from the perspectives of both companies, in terms of taxes paid, and governments, in terms of revenues received. The reconciliation of these two sets of accounts, which should obviously match up, is a valuable first step in fighting corruption relating to the oil, gas, and mining industries. For the data to be understood, it is up to NGOs, governments, and others to draw conclusions about what is really going on.

There is a growing trend toward "tell or explain why not" requirements in corporate responsibility reporting. Denmark was one of the first governments in the world to tell its large companies that they had to report on their non-financial performance, but it was up to them to say how they did it. In theory, the company could submit a piece of paper saying just "corporate responsibility has no relevance to my company." However, very few are brave or stupid enough to do this, even if they still wave a flag for Milton Friedman and believe this to be the case.

Similar requirements are now in place in a number of places around the world, ranging from the state of California, relating to trafficking and forced labor in supply chains, to China and the impacts of state-owned companies. For anyone who has read more than their fair share of CSR reports, and there were over 1,700 published in China in 2012 alone, they are a valuable first step, but are very much a first step.

However, there are a number of limitations to considering transparency in isolation from the substance of what is actually being disclosed:

First, companies measure their non-financial impacts in different ways and so comparisons between them are very tricky. Much more progress has been made on environmental aspects, and there are a number of very useful reporting standards that are used, including the Global Reporting Initiative, the principles of the World Resources Institute and the United Nations Global Compact, the United Nations Environment Programme Finance Initiative, and ISO 26000. Most of these standards also attempt to standardize the measurement of social impacts but with much less consistency. Most social indicators remain "process"-focused, that is, requiring that the company has the right system in place to deal with a risk or a potential negative impact, rather than a means of measuring the social impact itself. On the environmental side, it is a mix of both process and impact indicators that seems to work best, and efforts are under way to standardize social indicators in the same manner. This is hard work. Many social impacts are not as easily quantifiable as, for example, carbon dioxide emissions are, and even if they are measurable there still might be elements of subjectivity in the assessment (e.g. how do you know whether a human rights training program delivered by a company to its workers is of an excellent standard when the evaluation forms filled in by participants give a range of scores?). Measuring the success of a preventive social measure is even harder. How, for example, do you measure the absence of human rights abuse?

A second challenge is the fact that it is companies themselves that write these reports, albeit the figures and claims might be audited by a third-party organization. There are clearly resource reasons why this needs to be the case—it would be hugely unpopular for company Sustainability/CSR reports to be financed with tax-payers' money. However, it does, of course, allow the company (or whatever institution) to be selective about what they are going to be transparent about and the interpretation they place on specific pieces of data. This is not to say that companies lie in these reports, but there is certainly an element of "window dressing" in some of the best CSR reports and total "green-wash" in some of the worst.

Occasionally, companies will allow third parties to analyze their impacts with a freer hand. The two reports written by Oxfam focusing on the economic and social impacts of Unilever in Indonesia and Vietnam are seen as setting a new standard in transparency. However, to remain credible, Oxfam has written these reports without accepting any donation from Unilever, so there are financial constraints on how many such investigations any such NGO can do. Sometimes, a company will finance independent panels to investigate and report on controversial projects. One example of this was the report of the panel chaired by Senator George Mitchell on BP's Tangguh project in West Papua, but even here there were private and public components to the report. Companies such as Unilever and BP need to be commended for taking this second step toward transparency in reporting, where companies are willing not just to be a little more transparent, but also to allow others a free hand in interpreting what the data means—to take a stab at the truth. However, such reporting remains very much the exception, even for BP and Unilever, given the very many other operations both companies have, some considerably more controversial than those in the localities aforementioned. As mentioned earlier, BP might have been better served in the aftermath of the Gulf of Mexico disaster if it had been more transparent about the risks involved in deepwater drilling and how it was attempting to minimize them.

Accountability

In ethics and governance, accountability comprises answerability, blame-worthiness, liability, and the expectation of account giving. It is therefore central to our understanding of social license to operate to focus on the nature of the relationship between the license holder and those to whom they are answerable (or should be answerable). We can, and do, look to the law for legal accountability or to other professions, such as accountants and auditors, for institutional accountability. These traditional approaches will be examined in a while. It is clear, however, from arguments already made in this book, that institutional accountability needs to be understood in more fundamental terms than legal or fiduciary duties. Clearly accountability has a lot to do with power—we expect powerful organizations to be accountable even if we fear they might not be.

Between 2006 and 2008, the One World Trust issued a series of "Global Accountability Reports" which attempted to score different kinds of institution on indices of transparency, participation, evaluation, and compliance/response mechanisms.[6] As well as multinational companies, the research included intergovernmental organizations (IGOs) and international NGOs. Interestingly, there was no institutional category that outperformed the other as a whole, and there was significant variance within each category. IGOs and NGOs tended to be better at participation and evaluation, whist multinational companies tended to be better at responding to complaints. In terms of transparency it was actually the NGOs that were ranked, on average, the lowest. In a nutshell, the study showed that there are some businesses, IGOs, and NGOs that are accountable, and there are some that are much less so. It would be wrong to assume that an NGO is, by its mere nature and stated purpose, more accountable than a multinational corporation. However, it is clear from the perception of trust, discussed earlier in this book, that the general public does not tend to perceive institutions in this way. NGOs, particularly those with a popular cause or high-profile cause, will be trusted more than governmental institutions or businesses regardless of how accountable they are.

Thomas Paine's quote at the start of this chapter, whilst inspirational, is misleading. People do trust organizations and leaders even if some of them are very unaccountable. It is for this reason that trust is seen in this book as an underpinning concept for social license, whilst accountability is necessary for the latter's longer-term survival and growth. It is (unfortunately) not a prerequisite for the social license to exist. Again, the internet is a powerful example of this. Organizations that have a huge amount of power over our lives in cyberspace and who enjoy, today at least, relatively high levels of trust, have been subject to relatively little scrutiny until recently, and the accountability questions are still emerging following the Snowden revelations. In regard to any organization's longer-term survival, history would suggest that Paine's words are right: trust will eventually evaporate if adequate accountability mechanisms are not in place.

There might be several reasons for this: perhaps the age-old idea that we are all accountable to God and not to be held in judgment by each other, or the idea that we make lazy assumptions that leaders of organizations must be accountable to have risen to the level at which they stand. Yet the recent financial crisis in North America and Europe reminds us just how unaccountable some of society's most powerful organizations have been. For example, in 2013 a UK Parliamentary Committee concluded:

> Too many bankers, especially at the most senior levels, have operated in an environment with insufficient personal responsibility. Top bankers dodged accountability for failings on their watch by claiming ignorance or hiding behind collective decision-making... Ignorance was offered as the main excuse. It was not always accidental. Those who should have been exercising supervisory or leadership roles benefited from an accountability firewall between themselves and individual misconduct, and demonstrated poor, perhaps deliberately poor, understanding of the front line.[7]

The key message is that organizations should think about accountability much earlier in their activities and not shield senior management from knowledge of wrongdoing. Organizations can and do make early headway without adequate accountability, but this serves only to store up trouble for the future. Strong national legislation, such as the UK Bribery Act, which holds UK companies accountable for their activities worldwide, would not have been necessary if some UK companies had not been engaged in bribery overseas in order to win contracts. Their defense might be "other organizations do it [it is endemic in many countries], so why shouldn't a UK company also indulge in this practice if it is the price of doing business?" This is more or less the same defense that was given for the use of slaves 300 years ago.

The social contract is as much about justice-based as consent-based considerations as is social license. Social license without adequate attention to accountability will be lost eventually. It is just a question of when. Prime Minister Tony Blair was able to halt the investigations into BAE Systems' deal with the Saudi Kingdom but would a UK prime minister have the social, legal, or political license to do so again now? In 2013, the UK government was again presented with a complex dilemma when GlaxoSmithKline faced allegations of corruption in China, resulting in a 61 percent loss of sales in that market—potentially the world's largest.[8] This follows the same company pleading guilty to one of the biggest fraud cases against a company in US legal history in 2012 (the US is by far the biggest current market). Bribery and fraud are now illegal in many countries such as the UK, USA, China, and Saudi Arabia and the political will to hold companies to account seems to be increasing in some countries, reflecting an increasing intolerance of such practices by the public. Obviously there are countless political factors involved also, and the public will remain highly fickle in their perceptions. Indications are that social license in the future will not be sustained without adequate consideration of accountability.

Power imbalances can never be eradicated but, for social license to flourish, a number of steps can be taken:

- Knowledge of human rights risks and possible impacts—in particular on the least powerful—can be acquired and acted upon;
- Those lacking power can be incorporated in decision-making processes; the powerful can create participative processes that involve the poorest and most marginalized of rights-holders in a meaningful way;

- Transparency can help a lot but does not in itself compensate for inequalities of power unless information is both accessible and understandable;
- Finally, all organizations need to be accountable for their actions, and powerful organizations even more so. Impunity, perhaps more than any other issue, will weaken the social contract and destroy any social license. If the maxim that power is rarely given but most often taken holds, then this is where legislation is essential.

9

Prevention and remedies
Protecting victims and ensuring justice

"To whom then would I make the East India Company accountable? Why, to Parliament to be sure; to Parliament, from whom their trust was derived; to Parliament, which alone is capable of comprehending the magnitude of its object, and its abuse; and alone capable of an effectual legislative remedy."

Edmund Burke (1783)[1]

This chapter draws heavily on a previous publication I worked on with my colleague Haley St. Dennis at the Institute for Human Rights and Business and I would like to thank her, and the Institute, for allowing me to reproduce some of the material here, albeit in somewhat reworked form.[2]

As indicated in the previous chapters, ignorance of wrongdoing, of irresponsible behavior, or of negative social impacts should not be an acceptable defense, as it used to be for the leaders of large organizations. The indications are that the gap between "knew" and "should have known" will continue to narrow within the arena of both state and non-state accountability. A CEO might not be aware of significant social or environmental risks a company is taking, but they will be treated the same, whether or not they knew. They "should have known!" This chapter looks specifically at some recent developments in relation to legal mechanisms for holding business accountable for its human rights impacts and what conclusions might be drawn in relation to social license.

The *legal license* of any organization is not defined only by its commitments under national law but also by a growing body of international legal norms. The symbiosis between national and international law might be seen as a company's *legal license*. I would argue also that the absence of adequate legal mechanisms that reflect the interests of rights-holders and not just those of the organization itself can have a dramatic effect on the longer-term *social license*.

The analysis of this chapter shows how limited current law is in holding organizations accountable for their actions, particularly if those actions occur in another legal jurisdiction where local law, or local political will, might not allow a victim adequate access to remedy for a violation of what is an internationally recognized human right. There is clearly a need for much stronger and more effective legal remedies for the victims of abuse, as well as minimum standards for prevention.

Domestic adjudication over and sanctions for business involvement in human rights abuses are still underdeveloped. The basic components for an effective legal response are present in many countries, whether or not there is formal acceptance of concepts of corporate criminal liability, prosecution mechanisms, tort-based systems for non-criminal claims, or administrative sanction and fine systems. Many countries have explicitly criminalized the offences of genocide, war crimes, and crimes against humanity,[3] and implementation of the Rome Statute in many domestic penal codes expands the national incorporation of international crimes. These, though, are primarily aimed at individuals.

However, state frameworks for adjudicating criminal corporate involvement in human rights impacts are limited or non-existent in many states. Moreover, there is widely divergent state practice, as well as extensive practical, procedural, and extraterritorial barriers to the use of private or tort-based claims against companies, which have limited the success rate of cases. As a result, victims harmed by business activities around the world face huge obstacles in accessing adequate and effective remedies.

Access to justice

As the United Nations Guiding Principles on Business and Human Rights reaffirm, states have the duty to protect people against human rights violations within their boundaries, and to ensure that they have access to effective remedies. There are, however, often huge obstacles to victims in accessing justice for business-related impacts. The Protect, Respect, Remedy Framework itself notes this, stating:[4]

> Judicial mechanisms are often under-equipped to provide effective remedies for victims of corporate abuse. Victims face particular challenges when seeking personal compensation or reparation as opposed to more general sanction of the corporation through a fine or administrative remedies. They may lack a basis in domestic law on which to found a claim. Even if they can bring a case, political, economic or legal considerations may hamper enforcement.

The Guiding Principles call for states to address the legal, practical, procedural, and financial barriers preventing legal cases from being brought in situations where judicial resource is an essential part of accessing remedy, or alternative sources of effective remedy are unavailable.[5] As will be discussed below, however, variance in the way states approach criminal, civil, and administrative remedies for businesses' human rights-related impacts means that in some cases victims have one or more possible routes to obtain a remedy, and in other cases, none at all.

Consequently calls for an internationally legally binding mechanism to hold companies directly accountable, often raised before the 2005 initiation of the Special Representative on Business and Human Rights' mandate, were renewed in 2014 by a group of states, led by Ecuador and backed by dozens of NGOs.[6]

Criminal law

The Norwegian research foundation FAFO undertook a first-of-its-kind comparative survey in 2006 of the relevant national legislation in selected countries concerning businesses' liability under domestic civil and criminal law for the commission of, or complicity in, violations of international criminal and humanitarian law, both in and beyond national jurisdictions. It found a range of countries (usually civil law countries) that legally recognize the concept of corporate criminal liability, including Australia, Canada, the USA, South Africa, Norway, the Netherlands, the UK, Belgium, the Czech Republic, Italy, Luxembourg, Poland, Romania, the Slovak Republic, and Spain.[7]

Other countries, including France, explicitly recognize the concept of corporate criminal liability, but add a caveat with a list of exceptions to this general concept. Argentina, Indonesia, and Japan recognize corporate criminal liability only in relation to a specific list of offences contained in statutes and penal codes. More generally, states may impose criminal responsibility on a company for failing to act with due diligence to prevent certain crimes, which are often relevant to the protection of human rights, though not couched in rights-explicit terms. For example, these relate to environmental crimes that may threaten the right to life or health, violent crimes, and failures to prevent transnational bribery of public officials.[8]

In practice, the legal recognition of corporate criminal liability for human rights impacts is not being put to the test. Far more countries do not recognize the concept of corporate criminal liability than do. Moreover, although corporate criminal liability is theoretically possible in a number of states, attempted prosecutions of companies for human rights impacts are practically non-existent, though notable exceptions exist.[9] Indeed, most criminal cases against companies on human rights grounds are brought or instigated by NGOs and other representatives of victims, including lawyers who specialize in bringing this type of claim.[10] Country practices differ as to how actively involved victims can be in the investigation and prosecution after legal proceedings are initiated, as well as to how accountable to victims the prosecution will be. This could be due to a range of factors, including a lack of political interest and will to proceed with investigations and enforcement, and a lack of specific guidance or resources for prosecutors.

For example, the involvement of unscrupulous employers in violations such as forced labor or human trafficking is already a criminal offence in most jurisdictions, but there have been very few prosecutions of such businesses in most states. This disparity is compounded in an era when gross labor exploitation is recognized as a global problem with vulnerability in every state. Yet the lack of state-backed investigations shows that the current challenges extend beyond putting an appropriate legal framework in place, important as this step may be.

One extremely promising demonstration of state leadership and explicit uptake of the duty to protect against human rights abuses by business was recently laid before the French Parliament. In November 2013 MPs introduced a bill that would amend the penal and civil codes to require French companies to demonstrate that due diligence systems had been put in place as defined by the content of the UN Guiding Principles and OECD Guidelines. As noted in a recent update to a 2012 report on state regimes regarding due diligence by the International Corporate Accountability Roundtable (ICAR), the law would provide companies with a due diligence defense, noting: "The presumption of liability is not conclusive and the company may be exempt from liability if it proves that it was not aware of any activity that may have a potential impact on fundamental rights or if it proves that it made every effort to avoid it".[11] Moreover, the bill would amend the French Commercial Code to encourage monitoring of all activities that may impact fundamental rights, as well as to adjust these measures according to the means available to the company, enabling SMEs to implement measures according to their potential human rights impacts.[12]

Civil law

In addition to criminal law proceedings against businesses for human rights impacts, most countries allow civil law claims against businesses for harm or prejudice, as well as for failing to act with due diligence (known as tort law in common law jurisdictions and delict in civil law countries). Claimants using civil law approaches, however, tend to have to adapt their language and description of the impacts to fit certain legal definitions, such as "assault," "false imprisonment," or "wrongful death" (rather than human rights terminology such as "torture," "enslavement," or "genocide"). Clearly, such definitions do not always readily or adequately describe the severity of harms at issue in a human rights case.

While many states allow this use of civil law for alleged human rights impacts by businesses, there are big differences in countries' approaches to bringing such cases. This includes issues such as deciding on the forum to hear the case; the grounds for dismissal of a case; state immunity; the financing of such cases; the speed, efficacy, and competence of the court itself; rules around damage awards; investigation and enforcement across borders; and other political and procedural issues. This variance makes the private law approach a very unpredictable remedy option.

The US Alien Tort Claims Act (ATCA) has been the overwhelmingly dominant tort-based tool used globally to try to hold businesses accountable for human rights impacts. Historically, however, claims have rarely progressed beyond the procedural stage for the merits of the case to be heard in trial. Moreover, in April 2013, a US Supreme Court decision in *Kiobel v Royal Dutch Petroleum* curtailed the scope of the Act, and consequently the ability of non-US claimants to bring cases in the future involving business conduct occurring outside the USA or against non-US companies.[13] The decision does, for now, leave the door open to cases involving US companies, and potentially wider interpretations based on cases that "touch and concern" the USA. As a result, there are new initiatives created in the USA to spur on exploration of this new domestic legal landscape's potential and limits.[14]

There have been some promising recent developments within the civil law sphere in other jurisdictions—for example, in Uganda, where the High Court in Kampala recently found in favor of land tenants violently evicted by government forces in order for a coffee plantation to be developed, on the grounds that the Ugandan Investment Authority had failed to act with due diligence regarding the land transfer and community relocation.[15] Another recent judgment was in the Netherlands, where a Dutch court found a Nigerian subsidiary of Royal Dutch Shell negligent and liable for pipeline oil spills harming a Nigerian farmer, as a result of failing to take the precautionary measures necessary to reduce the risk to local people of sabotage to their operations (although the Court refused to rule on the explicit existence of a violation to their human rights due to a lack of precedent regarding a third party causing the harm.)[16]

The ability to bring civil claims is an indispensable avenue of redress for victims, but one where too few lawyers are willing to act given the costs and risks of litigation. States must not act in ways that further restrict access to such mechanisms, including within their legal aid programmes and other supportive measures. States should expect civil society organizations to continue to research and advocate expansion of the civil mechanisms available, as well as to experiment with new national and international avenues that have yet to be tested.

Administrative law

Germany, Italy, and Ukraine apply administrative penalties to companies. If found guilty, a company faces financial and other penalties. Within their administrative systems, states' explicit expectations of due diligence are proliferating. The most widespread practices regarding mandated due diligence are: environmental protection measures (over 130 countries are reported to have adopted an environmental assessment regime of one sort or another):[17] workplace health and safety due diligence (such as in Canada,[18] China,[19] and the Netherlands[20]); and the prevention of money laundering and illicit flows (such as in widespread state practice around "Know Your Customer" legislation).[21]

A promising development is found in the many countries which are developing deterrents in addition to financial penalties, such as restricting company operations in specific economic areas, banning them from procurement opportunities, publicizing convictions and penalties, and confiscating property in cases of breach of administrative regulations. Under the US Sentencing Guidelines, for example, companies can be put on probation, which requires proof of compliance with the law, combined with an ethics programme, as well as periodic reporting on their progress in implementing the designated reform program.[22]

As noted earlier, the USA has also mandated reporting for new investments in Myanmar (Burma) in relation to their human rights due diligence processes, as well as regarding supply chain due diligence in relation to conflict minerals sourced from the DRC. There are, however, few examples of other states clarifying within their administrative systems their human rights due diligence expectations of business. Making such clarifications will go a long way toward preventing human rights impacts in the first place, lessening the demand for the various judicial remedy options that have yet to provide sufficient access to justice for victims of business-related human rights impacts.

Extraterritoriality

States can exercise jurisdiction over activities occurring beyond their territorial boundaries under customary international law (though discussion of the complex nuances amongst the range of bases to do this falls outside the scope of this book).[23] At the same time, there are variations in state practice over extraterritorial jurisdiction regarding businesses' human rights impacts at a number of levels, both in regard to when they take a cross-border case and the extent to which they retain that jurisdiction through to its conclusion. There is even variation within a single state's practice, depending on the political implications of the case.[24]

This divergence leads to a great deal of uncertainty regarding access to judicial remedy outside the jurisdiction where the harm occurred, with the uncertainty itself becoming a barrier to victims' accessing of justice. Indeed, the United Nations' Protect, Respect, Remedy Framework notes:[25]

> Some complainants have sought remedy outside the State where the harm occurred, particularly through home State courts, but have faced extensive obstacles. Costs may be prohibitive, especially without legal aid; non-citizens may lack legal standing; and claims may be barred by statutes of limitations. Matters are further complicated if the claimant is seeking redress from a parent corporation for actions by a foreign subsidiary... These obstacles may deter claims or leave the victim with a remedy that is difficult to enforce.

The concept of separate corporate *personality* means than one member of a corporate group will not automatically be held legally responsible for the actions of another member. Using the corporate form can be a legitimate way of allocating and dividing risk to limit liability. There will, however, be times when there are grounds for "piercing the corporate veil" in order to hold the parent company liable for its involvement in or control over the acts of a subsidiary. Many jurisdictions are still working out their tests for determining when parent company involvement in or control over a subsidiary justifies looking to the parent rather than the subsidiary as the responsible party. Most domestic courts are wary of taking such action out of concern that they will undermine the concept of separate corporate personality.[26] As a result, it is only in very rare circumstances that parent companies have been held liable in their home jurisdiction for the actions of their overseas subsidiaries. This was seen, for example, in a major legal precedent set in the UK in 2012, when a parent company of a multinational

"only rarely have parent companies been held liable in their home jurisdiction for the actions of their overseas subsidiaries"

group was held accountable under the law of negligence for harms to the employees of one of its subsidiaries in South Africa.[27]

There are, however, many reasons why claimants may want to bring their human rights claims in another jurisdiction. Perhaps they have concerns over impartiality or the capacity of the local court to hear the claim in a timely way, or there may be more advantageous funding arrangements in another jurisdiction, access to more public interest lawyers and pro bono help, or there may be procedural advantages or greater scope for damage awards. Moreover, bringing a claim in the legal environment where the abuse occurred will not necessarily invoke a victim's confidence, whether for doubts in a court's capacity, lack of genuine political will to halt and remediate the harms, or fear of reprisal in bringing any claim at all.

As a result, there is evolving practice in terms of parent–subsidiary liability and expansive rules on jurisdiction regarding certain offences, extending the geographic reach of domestic law systems, such as in the UK, France, and Australia, where new theories are being developed based on a duty of care toward victims. This is a positive trend, and one that should be considered by all states to consolidate the reach of their human rights due diligence expectations of business, and not allow or enable the corporate form or chains of business relationships to be used to evade responsibility for impacts.

Extraterritoriality will continue to be one of the most vexing of state-to-state issues in terms of legal redress. It raises sensitive issues of sovereignty not just for the host state but also for the home state,[28] and is more complex than a global North–South dynamic as the number of transnational companies registered in key emerging economies continues to rise. Some encouragement can be drawn from non-legal extraterritorial cooperation, such as that relating to the OECD Guidelines on Multinational Enterprises, discussed further below.

Non-legal processes

Mediation is a central focus of National Contact Points (NCPs) in relation to the OECD Guidelines on Multinational Enterprises. Each OECD member, as well as a number of other affiliated governments in North Africa and

South America, is required to operate a non-legal national mechanism to hear complaints about companies wherever in the world they might be operating. In this way the mechanism is truly extraterritorial.

Since 2011, when the updated OECD Guidelines were put in place, human rights has emerged as a common denominator across nearly all the cases brought to NCPs by NGOs and communities, and to a lesser extent also by trade unions.[29] Whilst an increasing number of business sectors are the subject of cases, the extractive sector still dominates NCP activity and encompasses a broad range of geographic attention. Some NCPs attract more extractive sector-related cases than others (e.g. Australia, Argentina, Canada, Chile, the Netherlands, Norway, the UK, and the USA) given the composition of the industries in these countries. However, an increasing diversity of NCP cases can also be seen—the following NCPs have also been involved in recent cases: Belgium, Japan, Luxembourg, Mexico, Morocco, South Korea, and Switzerland.

Increasing collaboration between NCPs in relation to specific cases is also evident, as well as peer review and support more generally. Recently several NCPs have been reconstituted or strengthened in line with the updated Guidelines and national priorities. Other interesting trends include the growth of capacity in non-OECD countries that currently adhere to the Guidelines (such as a recent NCP conference in Brazil) and the development of parallel mechanisms in other economies (in India, for example).

Some states increasingly use NCPs strategically in their foreign policy. The Norwegian and UK NCPs have capacity-building agreements with the Brazilian NCP, and several NCPs have been engaged in peer review, for example the UK with Japan. Whilst such collaboration brings no direct commercial benefit, it does work toward creating a more level playing field for all OECD-based companies when working in key emerging markets. Another interesting example is the effort by the Italian NCP, together with the OECD Secretariat, to move toward much greater coherence in relation to the expectations of OECD-registered companies operating in Myanmar. States can also strengthen the leverage of NCPs by ensuring that there are economic consequences for businesses that are unwilling to enter into mediation and against whom they have issued a statement. The OECD "common approaches" for Export Credit Agencies require these agencies to take all NCP statements into account when considering whether to grant finance, and the Norwegian State Pension Fund has already cited NCP statements as a reason for divesting from certain companies.

Wider implications

As regards the legal accountability controls that states are able to exert over companies, these are often organized into three areas: administrative law, civil law, and criminal law, and sometimes a combination of the three. These legal controls relate to holding businesses to account for both their lack of measures to prevent harm to people, as well as to providing adequate remedies when businesses themselves cause, contribute to, or are linked to human rights impacts. Prevention and remedy are two fundamental legal functions—and human rights due diligence is relevant to both. The state needs to lead on initiating criminal law proceedings against companies when appropriate and under administrative law which is the basis for many discrimination, health and safety, and workplace rights cases. States also need to safeguard other legal avenues (administrative and civil) where the victims themselves, and not the state, must be the party to initiate action for harms caused. Site-level grievance mechanisms and state-level non-legal mechanisms also play an important role in addressing grievances before legal avenues become necessary. Providing and safeguarding access to legal remedy will always remain an essential part of any government's duty to protect human rights.

"prevention and remedy are two fundamental legal functions—and human rights due diligence is relevant to both"

The absence of adequate legal mechanisms is a *social license* as well as a legal license issue and will be increasingly so over the years ahead. It is important for any business to understand that there is likely to be a correlation over time between demonstrating due diligence and building trust through transparency and accountability on the one hand and diminishing liability and litigation risk on the other. Regardless of how the social license concept develops, my own view is that much stronger legal mechanisms will be needed beyond the initial steps set out in this chapter. But in turn, legal mechanisms will not be enough on their own to ensure social license.

Part 4

What Next?

10

Different organizations and the social license

"Manus Manum Lavat"
("One hand washes the other")

Lucius Annaeus Seneca (AD 54)[1]

Organizations whose primary purpose is not social

As discussed earlier in this book, not all organizations are part of the social contract in Hobbesian or Lockean terms. In other words, they do not represent the consent of the people in terms of the defense of their interests and their rights. For example, you would not look to your local supermarket to defend your human rights, not unless they have diversified into legal services (which some undoubtedly have). Rather, you would look to your government or the legal system it had created. However, you would expect any business to respect your human rights—to not infringe them. In other words, during your whole shopping experience, your entire relationship with the business in question, there should be no negative impact on your human rights. Most members of the public would not see this relationship in human rights terms. They would understand it as "consumer rights"—including issues such as data protection (right to privacy), good labeling (right to information), and protection from being poisoned (right to health). The global standard of non-infringement, of respecting human rights, is now a global standard for all businesses worldwide, and can be taken to be our benchmark for all types of non-state actor.

So, if classic social contract theory might not apply to non-state actors in the same way as it does to state actors, it nevertheless remains relevant. If we accept that the social license is a modern manifestation of the social contract, and—very importantly—one that relates to an activity and not directly to the existence of an organization, then we have a historical basis for starting to understand social license. Whilst a growing number of companies have started to explore the social license concept, very few of them have done so through the lens of the social contract, as I have endeavored to do in this book. As argued earlier, this exploration requires companies to look at both the consent and justice elements of the social license, which are missing from much of what has previously been written on the social license.

As to why a business might need social license for an activity, this should also be evident by this stage in the book. With modern technology, and resurgent awareness of local and national identity in an otherwise globalizing world, it seems that individuals, communities, NGOs, and others are willing to show their displeasure at activities in which they feel they have no stake, or about which they have not been consulted, or which have been delivered by organizations they do not trust or see as legitimate. Communities are also looking for greater equity and justice before granting social license. Issues such as the living wage, CEO pay, corruption, workplace harrassment, discrimination, and health and safety are now seen as global and not just national or regional issues. More than at any other time in history perhaps, consumers are starting to realize their own stake in how things currently are—how buying jeans at $5 or $10 a pair must relate in some way to very poor working conditions in Bangladesh—and the collapse of buildings killing 1,100 mainly young female workers, the same age and gender as most of those buying the jeans around the world.

"communities are also looking for greater equity and justice before consenting to a social license"

It is easy to overstate the leverage that social license actually has today. Few companies have gone out of business yet because their social license has been withdrawn. There are indications that the social license will be become a much more tangible concept for businesses in the years to come. It already is for many in the mining sector (where communities and businesses have a very proximate and physical relationship). It is no accident that the concept started in the mining sector, but it seems highly likely that it will be on the lips of executives from a broad range of business sectors over the years ahead.

Who will shape the social license of business?

Businesses themselves can help to shape the way the concept of social license develops over the years ahead, but only if they have the legitimacy, trust, and consent to do so. Whether businesses engage in the process or not, it will happen for one or more of the following reasons.

Communities will demand it

Communities will demand a greater stake in the decision-making processes relating to major extractive or infrastructure projects that have an environmental or social impact. Indications are that if the global price of oil and gas continues to slide downwards, then onshore exploration will define the future of the industry more than offshore exploration for the next decades. Added to this is the preference for gas over oil (partly for climate change reasons), with much more invasive effects on the landscape (shale gas or coal-bed methane fracking, for example). We are likely to see the oil and gas industries facing the kind of questions those in mining have faced for several years now. Think also of other large infrastructure projects and how communities engage in them. The stalling of the CPI Yunnan Hydropower project in Myanmar,[2] for example, shows that Chinese companies are facing the social license issues as much as any Western company.

However, there are some dangers ahead, as the current fracking debate in the UK and elsewhere has reminded us—the consent of communities has largely been overlooked by both governments and business. The exception is the "free, prior, and informed consent" of indigenous peoples. Most governments outside of Latin America have not committed themselves to this standard either in binding international law, even if they have agreed to it in spirit. But don't all communities deserve some meaningful notion of consent? This is more than just being listened to in a consultation process. As this book has already explored, the public is used to being asked for its consent in relation to a number of other business activities, so why not in relation to a major project on a community's own doorstep?

It is likely that through the use of social media and through the involvement of outside NGOs, local communities around the world will increasingly ask for their voices to be listened to and for their consent to be requested in a free, prior, and informed manner. This is, of course, very different from giving local communities an automatic veto. "Nimbyism" is not in the interests of poor communities, much as it stymies development and business. Indigenous peoples require special protection in relation to consent but even for them its withholding is not an absolute veto either, albeit the process for overriding local sentiment is not adequately in place and is certainly not rights-based in most countries. Nevertheless, communities will demand consent and it is in everyone's interest to try to achieve this. I see no legitimate claim to social license if the issue of consent is not squarely dealt with.

Investors will ask for proof of it

Earlier in this book I looked briefly at some of the thinking emerging in the investment community about creating greater economic leverage for socially responsible investors. Some, such as Al Gore and David Blood, hope to use their holdings in companies to influence commitment to climate change. In the USA, for example, the heavy lifting by investors on climate change is being done via Ceres/INCR and the Carbon Disclosure Project (and those such as Bennett Freeman at Calvert Investments) and by plenty of other investors. It seems increasingly likely that the trend in many stock markets around the world to integrate sustainability issues—including aspects of social license—will continue and, similarly, an increasing number of investors will see environmental and social issues as material in their own right, as well as being a good proxy for sound management in general. It is indeed pertinent to ask why businesses should be valued on assets listed on a balance sheet today that they will not be able to exploit due to the social and environmental expectations of tomorrow. An asset for which a business has lost its social license is stranded unless the business looks to the courts or the police/military to enforce its legal or political license for a specific activity. Many businesses might still choose to do so, but they should end all their "social claims" if they do, with the likely knock-on effects on perceived legitimacy, trust, and consent elsewhere in the world.

Another arena in which social license might begin to have a measurable commercial value is that in which companies (or their assets) are bought, sold, or merged. Mergers and acquisitions lawyers (M&A lawyers) are generally not given to flights of fancy or spin (note the deadpan use of the word "disposals" for company assets that are sold). For M&A lawyers to talk in social license terms would indeed be an indicator of progress for the concept.

In this book I have already looked at the example of oil and gas exploration in East Africa and the way that many of the (often small) onshore exploration companies still operate below the radar of public or political attention. There is at present no business case for these companies to engage in human rights due diligence and very little binding legislation which requires them to do so. Both of these are needed for behavior to change. What if an exploration company does spend a serious amount of money and time in developing good community relations during the community phase, insuring that the process is indeed "free, prior, and informed," and what if the company does undertake thorough social impact assessments and does publish some or all of its findings—what then? We can take the cynical position that no company will really be serious about doing so. Even binding legislation will not influence and change behavior on its own to a sufficient extent. A mix of stick and carrot is needed.

At the moment "political risk" is a category that most M&A lawyers are familiar with, and when exploration companies sell up to the "majors," prices can be discounted (sometimes very significantly) if the assets are threatened by instability, violence, or unrest. This is a negative indicator that absence of social license is already integrated to some extent into the process. However, there is no positive equivalent—no value for social license—when it exists in relation to a business project. It seems unlikely, perhaps undesirable, that there should be any fixed metric for measuring social license. It is, as we are now well aware, a highly contextualized and time-bound thing. Its mere articulation in formal terms can act to diminish it. However, a valuation as part of an acquisition process is also a contextualized and time-bound process—a price is agreed at a single point in time.

There are a small number of oil and gas exploration companies which are actively interested in what this might mean within the context of East Africa. The impact of getting it wrong—or losing social license—is apparent in many parts of the continent, not least the delta area of Nigeria. However, Africa also holds nuggets of good practice: the social license has been maintained and built upon in Botswana, Ghana, and Liberia. How the oil and gas sector will be perceived by communities in Uganda, Kenya, or Tanzania is currently to play for, or more accurately, to work for. If the consent and trust of communities can be maintained, then perhaps—just perhaps—social license will have a commercial value for specific discovery sites when junior exploration companies come to sell their discoveries to larger operators over the years to come. This is one context where we will be able to judge whether the social license is a meaningful concept. However, the challenges are immense. Take Kenya as an example. Oil has been discovered in the far north of the country around Lake Turkana, an area where many communities do not feel they are part of Kenya, and therefore will not take the legitimacy of either state or non-state actors for granted. Add to this the security challenges facing the country in relation to neighboring countries such as Somalia or South Sudan—not to mention the internal ethnic and religious tensions—and we begin to see why the social license concept is so important and also why it is so important to get right.

Another arena in which social license might start to have direct commercial value in the near future is information and communication technology. Whilst consent is a legal responsibility for internet service providers in most countries, the consent that consumers give is largely tacit. Very few bother to read the small print relating to the protection of their privacy. The big moments of revelation have yet to come—when companies such as Facebook or Google are sold and so too all that data about us: our shopping patterns, our social preferences, and so on. There is, at present, a very high level of trust between the public (and it really is the public in most countries, as we are nearly all consumers of the internet) and the companies involved.

This trust can be shaken and was shaken when the Edward Snowden revelations showed that these same companies had been handing over personal data to the US intelligence agencies such as the National Security Agency (NSA). Companies have always handed over data to the government in accordance with the law. Now the norm is that a proper legal request is made through the proper channels and some companies then report those numbers in transparency reporting. What happened here was either that secret services were collecting data without the companies' knowledge (though companies deny that the NSA had direct access to their servers for the Prism project) by intercepting data being transmitted between servers or putting taps on undersea cables carrying internet traffic, or that the NSA was serving companies with blanket orders to hand over ALL consumer data, and the companies weren't allowed to reveal that they had been told to do this. This made a mockery of transparency reporting.

So where is the commercial value? Well, interestingly, during the last few months of 2013, Deutsche Telekom's number of German subscribers increased significantly, with the company commenting:

> Germans are deeply unsettled by the latest reports on the potential interception of communication data. Our initiative is designed to counteract this concern and make email communication throughout Germany more secure in general. Protection of the private sphere is a valuable commodity.[3]

So the protection of consumer privacy arguably already has a commercial value, and this is likely to be more and more the case in years to come:

> "The revelations from Edward Snowden were certainly a wake-up call," said Thomas Kremer, Board member for Data Privacy, Legal Affairs and Compliance at Deutsche Telekom. "Going forward, we need to keep our eyes wide open. Politics, business and science now need to work out solutions".[4]

If ICT companies want to maintain the relatively strong social license they currently enjoy, then there will be some harder choices for them over the years ahead. If they insist that consumers use their true names and identity details, consumers will need increased assurance that their data will be protected. This was not the case in countries such as Egypt or Bahrain in recent years, and was not the case for Chinese journalists using

Yahoo email in years past. Those companies best able to maintain freedom of expression whilst protecting personal privacy will be those likely to be most trusted, and the consent granted to them will be less tacit and more likely to be informed. German consumers are amongst the most discerning in the world. This might be the start of a trend.

Consumers will start to take a more active interest

The Deutsche Telekom example above is an early example of what might become a broader trend. However, so far the evidence generally is that consumers remain a generally fickle group of stakeholders. The data relating to the level of trust in brands, examined in Chapter 5, suggests that many other factors are involved in the way that consumers regard whole industries, as well as specific brands. There are many reasons why consumers don't have a well informed approach to what they buy. Many consumers, even now, don't really care about the social performance of a company. The boycott of specific companies or specific products is not often a decisive factor in company performance, though there have been some notable exceptions to this through history. It should be noted also that in competitive and highly branded markets, where market share is tight and brands are a huge part of the value of the overall company, even small changes in buying behavior can have a big influence.

The needle of consumer apathy is shifting, albeit slowly. Clearly on issues such as product quality—in particular for foodstuffs or medicine—poor company performance can destroy both market share and social license, whether it be counterfeit pharmaceutical products in Nigeria, milk contamination in China, or horse meat in the UK. There is also the notorious "Ratner case" where the founder and CEO of a low-cost jewelry company mocked his own consumers on a TV show and was out of business within months—not for any legal or political reason, but through loss of social and then economic license. So there are some reasons to believe that consumers might become an influence in social license issues. At least for the coming years and for most companies (particular those whose brands are completely unknown to the consumer), this type of influence will only be marginal.

Governments will mandate some aspects of social license

I have argued in this book that social license cannot take the form of a formally written agreement, and also that it is not an alternative to strong laws and good relationships. Therefore, if a government required by law that a company always maintained social license, it would be a contradiction in terms. It would in effect become a legal license issue. This is not a rare occurrence—it happens all the time—an issue of how an organization behaves is one day not legally required and then the next day becomes a legal requirement. However, it would be a serious mistake therefore to think of social license as only a voluntary concept—as something such as "self-declaratory CSR." It can be, and should be, a much deeper concern than this. I predict that many of the human rights requirements of companies that are today non-binding, will become binding in the future. They will become part of the legal license that all companies will need to have to operate. This does not negate the concept of social license. In fact it strengthens it, as the law can only ever do so much to influence behavior. Greater transparency, greater accountability, and greater access to justice for victims can—and should—receive greater legal backing around the world. But it is the net effect of these, as well as a range of other considerations (such as "trust" and "legitimacy") which cannot be easily defined in law, that represents the social license.

Therefore, we are likely to see governments making what are component parts of the social license legal requirements. Evidence of this is already emerging, and examples have been given earlier in this book. Recent moves on making disclosure and reporting on the social impacts of business a legal requirement are a good start, as is a focus on full supply chain transparency in industries (such as "conflict minerals"), on issues (such as human trafficking and forced labor), and in countries (such as Myanmar). Whilst trust and legitimacy cannot be mandated, greater transparency and accountability can, and these efforts will make social license a more central concern for business generally.

Organizations whose primary purpose is social

There are a range of organizations whose primary stated purpose is social (not economic or political), ranging from community-based organizations (CBOs) to international NGOs. Many of these organizations would see themselves as integral to the social contract between individuals within society itself, and hence the term "civil society" organizations. However, if an organization defines itself as representing civil society, this does not mean that questions of legitimacy do not arise.

For CBOs, legitimacy comes from their relation to a specific, geographically defined, group of people to whom the organization needs to be accountable. As already discussed in this book, consent is key to the social license. It is central to the way that other organizations need to relate to CBOs, whether it be a business planning a project, a government clearing land, or an international NGO claiming to represent their interests. But consent is not enough—justice-based considerations are also important. The CBO needs processes in place to ensure that it is indeed representative of those it claims to represent. Does it represent the full community? Does it adequately represent the interests of women, of the young, or of minorities within the community? It is not uncommon for the answer to this question to be "no." It would be short-sighted of CBOs to think that social license is just something for businesses to worry about, that it is something that they can give consent to but is not directly their concern. This comes into focus when parallel CBOs emerge to compensate for the lack of representation of certain individuals or groups.

NGOs need also to consider the social license for their activities and not make any easy assumptions. It might be that the category of "social purpose" organizations in a particular country is a wide one and full of historical anachronism. For example, it was only relatively recently that UK charity law was amended to allow human rights organizations charity status, provided they were non-partisan politically. However, private schools have enjoyed charity status for 200 years with the associated privilege of not having to pay any business or corporation tax to the government. This makes sense in historical terms, as many private schools were established to educate some of the most disadvantaged in British (mainly English) society. However, many of these same schools now educate the elite within British society and have little to do with the socially marginalized, yet they maintain their charity status. A recent survey of the British class system defined the "elite"—the top 6 percent of British society—as likely to have attended private schools.[5] They are also most likely to have senior positions in organizations. So I need to be careful I do not provoke too many of its readers on this point! The issue is not to take a position on private schooling in the UK. Rather, it is that organizations founded with a social purpose might not always be seen to be legitimate in these terms by others in the same society.

Another example is the position of international NGOs operating on global issues. It is still the case that the majority of international NGOs are based in the global North or in OECD member countries, particularly in Northern Europe and North America. This dynamic is starting to change. Human rights organizations, such as Conectas (based in Brazil), Al Haq (in Palestine), and BRAC (in Bangladesh), are becoming key regional and global players, but it is still true that most of the best-known NGOs, from Greenpeace (based in Amsterdam) to Amnesty International (based in London), and from Oxfam (based in Oxford) to Human Rights Watch (based in New York), are based in the global North. There are currently 3,900 NGOs that have "consultative status" with the United Nations. Some countries are much more represented in the list than others, and it certainly does not reflect the global population, which would suggest that two-thirds of these NGOs should either be Chinese or Indian.

This book has already commented on the fact that although CBOs are likely to draw their legitimacy from who they are as much as what they do, NGOs draw much more from their purpose and their activities than they do from their rationale for existing or from governance arrangements. However, these remain live issues for any international NGO.

The existentialist challenge that many NGOs have is that the majority of their financial support, whether from individual members, supporters, governments, or private foundations, comes from the global North, whilst the majority of their work and delivery is focused on the global South. Twenty years ago this was less of a problem, at least in development terms, as that is where the money was. As the money shifts to emerging economies, will the NGO supporter base shift in a similar way? Perhaps it will. What is not certain is whether it will be the same NGOs that will represent these interests. Will NGOs such as Amnesty International and Friends of the Earth be able to replicate in China and India (and in population terms vastly outperform) their historic memberships in Northern Europe and North America? Will Greenpeace or Human Rights Watch find the same rich private donors and other supporters in Beijing, Shanghai, Delhi, Mumbai, Rio, São Paulo, or Moscow that they have in London or New York? Does it matter?

I contend that it does. Whilst international NGOs draw a lot of their legitimacy from their activities, by which they work to realize global norms relating to development goals, climate change, human rights, humanitarian law, and so on, who they are also matters. If they are perceived as "foreign organizations" with little local support, their activities might be constrained. If they do not enjoy social license, they are more vulnerable to the whims of government and other powerful interest groups that might not align with all of their campaigning objectives. I realized this myself the day I gave a 30-minute keynote speech to the president of a key emerging economy—a constructive and diplomatic speech on human rights and business in his country. The speech was well received, but the president's response was interesting. He took the opportunity not so much to respond to any of my individual points, but rather to respond to the general (mainly environmental) criticism he was aware his country felt when NGO experts arrived from London or Washington to deliver their concerns. At that moment, and to that audience, the fact that my organization had worked in his country for several years with strong local partnership mattered. However, I was still a foreign voice speaking on domestic considerations. Ethiopia has gone still further to restrict the activities of foreign-funded NGOs, whilst laws against homosexuals in Uganda are actively supported by religious NGOs funded, in part, by Christian fundamentalists in the USA.

This is not finger-pointing. We need to remember which government's agents (the French blew up a Greenpeace ship docked in New Zealand in 1985[6]), or which governments are alleged to have infiltrated direct-action NGOs to the extent of getting undercover police to form sexual relationships with key activists.[7] If we accept that one of the new frontiers for many NGOs is cyberspace, then the gloves are off in the way that many security agencies in several countries use mass and targeted surveillance to eavesdrop on NGOs and CBOs. It must be remembered that civil society organizations include those that have strong opinions on religion and conflicts in other parts of the world, or discriminate against its supporter basis, or are explicitly anti-immigrant or promote other types of hatred. Mitigating the spread of hate speech, including incitement to violence, and engaging in child protection processes/procedures are legitimate roles for private companies and governments, and so the balance

"civil society remains a contested space everywhere. For this reason alone, social license matters"

between freedom of expression, privacy, and the protection of the population is a complex one and one which requires much more attention globally.

Civil society remains a contested space everywhere. For this reason alone, social license matters. NGOs must constantly be aware of where they draw their legitimacy from—how much from their organizational basis and how much from activities. These factors will change through time. NGOs must constantly challenge themselves in terms of their purpose and whose interests are they serving. Is it to protect the environment, the poor, or human rights defenders? And do NGOs choose activities to resonate with their supporter base, other donors, or the media? If an NGO's supporters are not a diverse group but predominantly of a particular age, religion, ethnicity, or nationality, how can the NGO ensure that this bias does not infringe on how it engages in what are global norms?

International NGOs need social license as much as any business does. Legitimacy, trust, and consent cannot be assumed just because an organization is part of global civil society. Local social license can buy an NGO protection against local interests that might try to undermine their license to operate. If the British or Dutch secret service stormed and closed down the offices of Amnesty International or Greenpeace in London or Amsterdam, there would be public and political outcry. Similar acts in other countries would prompt a more muted response.

It is not just in London that libel law has been used by powerful interests to try to stifle freedom of expression. In India, many NGOs have been threatened by lawsuits for speaking out. One leader of a Dutch worker rights NGO even had an Interpol arrest warrant taken out against her for allegedly defaming a specific company. And, of course, there are reasons why many human rights organizations still have their East Asian offices in Hong Kong and not in Beijing. Moscow too remains a hostile place for some NGO activities, particularly those working on gay and lesbian rights.

What about governments?

Governments are, at least according to social contract theory, the creation of the social contract between individuals in any society, whether this be an authoritarian government (such as Hobbes' *Leviathan*) or one rooted in consultative democracy (such as Rousseau's *New Republic*). Clearly not everyone sees governments in such contractual terms and the legitimacy of states can be defended in other historical, military, and cultural foundations. However, democracy has become a relatively persuasive foundation for state legitimacy over recent decades, and therefore contract theory retains a central space in the way we understand how states derive their own legitimacy. Whilst non-state actors derive much of their legitimacy from their activities, states rarely do so. Traditionally it is enough for a government to win an election and abide by (or change) the state's constitution (if it has one). So why should a government take any interest in the social license?

I have given a number of examples as I unpacked what the social license is, or why it does have direct relevance to states. Even if governments draw most of their legitimacy from what the state is, they are finding it necessary to legitimize specific activities beyond the normal wheels of representative democracy. Communities, interest groups, NGOs, and online activists are demanding a greater say in key decisions that might, in the past, have been purely the prerogative of elected officials with their political license. Special commissions have been set up; constitutions have been amended; and laws have been framed based on direct government–public interaction, which to some extent bypasses elected officials and the legislature, at least initially.

Take for example the UK Government's website for citizen petitions to put forward or abolish existing laws. Countries, such as Switzerland, or states, such as California, that allow citizens to promote and vote on issues directly, have seen an upsurge in activity over recent years. Some national leaders have been keen to push citizens to focus on their own responsibilities and not just their rights, in the way that President Kennedy famously did in his inaugural speech of 1961.[8] These are very much social contract type questions, but ones which relate to the contract between the state and the individual. International human rights law, for example, looks to the state and its duties. People have rights, but their duties to each other are very much mediated by the state itself. When politicians have tried to get citizens to think about their own responsibilities to each other, the plea has often fallen on deaf ears—for example, Prime Minister Cameron in the UK and his "big society" concept. In a way, the state has been so successful as a concept that it makes citizens unwilling to think of their own direct responsibilities to each other. One exception was Prime Minister Major's "Citizen's Charter" which was partially successful in promoting some clarity on the how social contracts might be made more explicit in today's society.

Indications are, however, that the social contract is re-emerging as a legitimate way of thinking about both state and non-state actors. The internet again is a classic example of this, in that the last thing most online users want is the creation of a "Leviathan" for the internet, even if this is based within the United Nations. "Web neutrality" is a key concept and social activists prefer to see the internet in "global commons" terms, with the need for strong rules that can be established and policed by a multitude of actors, amongst which the state is just one. The Edward Snowden revelations about the US National Security Agency, as well as the issues that Yahoo faced in China, remind us that states—or at least some parts of government—will resist seeing the internet as a new form of social contract. The governance of the internet, and the activities of state and non-state actors in cyberspace, will remain a defining issue of the next decade. It is a discussion in which the social license of governments has some meaning.

It is also important to remind ourselves that states are not just legislators or defenders of security and rights. They are also powerful economic actors in their own right. A few years ago it might have been felt that state-owned enterprises were a thing of the past, but it is predicted that they will remain dominant players in most national and international economies for the whole of this century. The question then becomes: in whose interests does a state-owned enterprise act—the state's, or its own? Can it be seen as having a social purpose? Is it part of the social contract and to what extent does it need social license for its activities? It is interesting in itself that there is no international consensus on the answers to these questions. Some governments see the companies they own very much as extensions of sovereign power and control, others as companies that the state just happens to have invested in (to bail out, as in the case of failing banks, to show national economic pride, or to make a healthy return). The European Court of Human Rights seems to suggest that it is the function that a business undertakes that determines whether it should have the same duties as the state, whilst such discussions within the OECD and the United Nations seem to focus more on the ownership of the company.

The fact that the UK bank which currently has my personal account is mainly state-owned has not really changed my expectations of it. If anything, it might have increased them. If the bank needed social license before the scandals of recent years, it most certainly needs it now. Arguably, the nationalization of banks was in part related to their loss of social license—a failure of trust and legitimacy—as well as financial failure. Some of the failing banks, at least the smaller ones, could have been acquired by non-failing private banks. But was there any social license to do so at that time, or is there still sufficient social license for a small number of large banks to dominate the market, particularly when some of them are state-owned?

State ownership provokes some interesting questions, as do other ways in which the state uses economic leverage over private actors. Public procurement, for example, can amount to around 20 percent of GDP in many counties: the conditions a government puts on what it buys, and from whom, can have profound economic consequences. It is not often an issue for election campaigns or manifestos, but rather much an administrative decision based on the economic interests of the state, as are the financial incentives governments give to their companies to invest abroad and in particular countries. Sovereign wealth funds are another example: organizations investing in many parts of the world— whether it be Gulf State funds buying up land in Africa or the Norwegian Pension Fund investing or divesting from companies based on its social criteria. The German government has strong supply chain interests for raw materials in countries such as Kazakhstan and Mongolia, as does the French government for uranium in Niger, for example.

It is when we think about the activities of a state in other parts of the world, sometimes acting for political, economic, or social interests—or a combination of all three—that we can see that governments too need to consider their social license. This is perhaps most explicit in discussions relating to the internet, where civil society takes a very libertarian non-state intervention line, but it is also true in some of the states' other activities.

One example of implicit state and non-state recognition of the social license is the National Contact Point system under the OECD Guidelines for Multinational Enterprises. (It also reminds us that the consequences for those willing to defy the very idea of such social responsibilities remain weak at present.) Through this, NGOs, trade unions, communities, and even other companies can bring complaints for mediation by state officials (or their appointees) from either the home or host government, after which states can issue public statements, including statements critical of those concerned. The fact that these procedures have no legal consequences means that they rely almost exclusively on social license criteria, with the possibility that the state might use its economic power to put pressure on companies unwilling to engage in mediation.

Whilst the system is far from perfect, the fact that it exists at all (and now in 42 countries) is significant. Some would say it is a fig leaf used by governments to prevent them from having to do more in relation to the legal license of the companies concerned. That is too simplistic a dismissal. As argued before, such mechanisms do not replace legal action or other mechanisms. They in fact make access to justice more likely over the longer term, partly by highlighting where access to justice is frustrated or denied. Fundamentally, these mechanisms break new ground as they illustrate the transnational and supranational nature of the social license: transnational because both home and host states have an interest in how non-state actors behave and supranational because they reinforce the fact that legitimacy and social license have to be considered within the context of international norms. The last chapters of this book reflect on the need for more such multi-stakeholder partnerships over the years ahead, on the ways in which social license can be a tool for achieving greater accountability, and finally on what the social license might mean for the rest of this century.

chapter 11

A basis for partnership and accountability

"Where, after all, do universal human rights begin? In small places, close to home—so close and so small that they cannot be seen on any maps of the world. Yet they are the world of the individual person; the neighbourhood he lives in; the school or college he attends; the factory, farm or office where he works. Such are the places where every man, woman and child seeks equal justice, equal opportunity, equal dignity without discrimination. Unless these rights have meaning there, they have little meaning anywhere. Without concerned citizen action to uphold them close to home, we shall look in vain for progress in the larger world."

Eleanor Roosevelt (1958)[1]

This planet, and the 7 billion people on it, face some big challenges, the challenges of climate change; poverty; fundamentalism (of all kinds); gender, social, and economic marginalization; human rights abuses; resource scarcity; human migration; privacy and freedom on the internet; global health; biodiversity; and the rights of all. None of these issues can be addressed effectively unless enough state and non-state actors align and work together. Whilst much is wrong with the world, there is some good news. The way that unlikely coalitions have eventually come together over recent years to fight against problems such as HIV/AIDS, malaria, and landmines, and to fight for issues such as maternal health, female education, and health and safety—this is encouraging. Encouraging too is that the majority of governments around the world would today recognize that they owe their existence to at least some element of democracy and a social contract with their people, rather than seeing it as the divine will of god or as a hereditary right.

It has been estimated that the world will need another $1 trillion of investment to meet new 2015 UN Development Goals and that this needs to come from partnerships between governments and the private sector.[2] However, relatively little attention has been given to what makes such partnerships accountable and legitimate. Do such partnerships have social license? Do they need it? Is the social license a means to an end, or are there some partnerships that are about the creation of social license itself?

The challenges faced by existing partnerships

Let's take the United Nations as an example. Some UN agencies, such as WHO and UNICEF, have been central to the development of many effective partnerships, and most UN agencies have their own policies for the creation, development, and evaluation of partnerships with each other, with governments, with civil society, and with business. The Secretary-General's office has its own history of partnerships, one of the most relevant to the issues raised in this book being the UN Global Compact created in 1999. However, there is still no standard framework for how the UN administers these partnerships, and in particular, no shared mechanism for ensuring their accountability.

The issue is more fundamental. The fact that the world has such pressing needs can seem to give sufficient social license for a range of partnership to address them. Why get tied up in complex and esoteric discussions about governance, reporting, and transparency, when it is the practical impact that really matters?

Similar tensions exist in multi-stakeholder approaches outside of the UN. The Kimberley Process on tackling conflict diamonds and the Voluntary Principles on Security and Human Rights were two early attempts, initiated around the turn of the millennium. Both have been challenged on questions of governance as well as on their practical effectiveness.

The existence of a plethora of Multi-Stakeholder Initiatives (MSIs) in the apparel sector (Ethical Trading Initiative, Fair Labor Association, Social Accountability International, Fair Wear Foundation, and so on) did not prevent the Rana Plaza disaster in 2013 and the death of over 1,100 workers, or the previous fires in Bangladesh and Pakistan—even when one of the factories had been certified by one of the MSIs in question.

Yet there are a growing number of MSIs being created, even though it takes enormous efforts to do so. The Global Network Initiative (GNI) was established in 2008 to deal with some of the internet dilemmas faced by companies such as Google, Microsoft, and Yahoo, but the mobile operators would not join at this point. There have been some recent attempts to set objective criteria for measuring the performance of MSIs,[3] but this is very tricky, not least because the very existence of these initiatives owes so much to both political and social license.

The issues that MSIs face are profound—whether it be the exploitation of labor deep within supply chains, the behavior of state or private security forces in remote areas, or the demands of security services in relation to the internet. In many cases, the foreign ministries of governments do not have sight of what other government departments are demanding of companies and NGOs. Sometimes whole industries are divided between companies that want the MSI to become stronger and more effective in terms of accountability; others who prefer the status quo; NGOs that believe that MSIs can really have impact and change the behavior of governments and companies; and others who are cynical that they are little more than "green-" or "blue-washing."

Yet despite the odds being stacked against them, MSIs have continued to emerge over the past 15 years. This is perhaps in large part due to the fact that despite their many flaws and the messiness of multi-stakeholder engagement, they are the only show in town for bringing different state and non-state actors to the table to tackle complex international social issues. Even those who think that firmer regulation is needed find it difficult to see how some element of "multi-stakeholderism" is not needed to actually make complex things happen in practice. It might be concluded that MSIs are a good incubator for the development of stronger laws—such as the US government has developed in relation to transparency in the extractive industry (despite or because of the existence of the Extractive Industries Transparency Initiative or the Kimberley Process). As discussed earlier in this book, any initiatives based on prevention (including laws that require it) need to be calibrated in terms of due diligence criteria that are actually implementable. However, there is a general frustration that the partnerships that sit behind MSIs cannot achieve more for the human rights and livelihoods of the vulnerable individuals and communities in question.

Can social license help to develop more effective and stronger partnerships?

Could social license be an effective concept for better and more effective partnerships? There are some real challenges about discussing multi-stakeholder partnerships in social license terms that might be summarized as:

- Stakeholders will have varying perceptions of the legitimacy of such initiatives and partnerships themselves—and these will vary within the organizations. With a few exceptions, political leaders and CEOs are not directly involved, partly because they have not been central to the social license of companies in a general sense. However, it can be argued that this situation is changing. Given the importance of the Code of Conduct relating to private security companies as well as the Global Network Initiative, it might be seen as having an "existentialist" aspect for the companies involved.
- The public, consumers, and politicians are largely unaware of these partnerships. They are more aware of those that are remedial—such as those aimed at meeting global development goals—than those that are preventative; or agreeing and implementing adequate levels of due diligence. The impact of the latter is much harder to demonstrate in tangible terms. Partnerships, therefore, need strategies for developing much wider social license than has been the case in the past.

• Finance is a critical concern. Is it legitimate for civil society organizations or United Nations agencies to be cross-funded in such partnerships by businesses and, if so, what accountability mechanisms need to be put in place? The partnership between Oxfam and Unilever in Indonesia and Vietnam, where Oxfam received no funding from Unilever, is a much more credible model than those funded or sponsored by business. Sometimes businesses can fund reports that are respected: UNEP's report on Ogoniland in Nigeria is an example of this, or the various WHO reports on communicable diseases.

It should be expected that partnerships developed to achieve social goals also develop social license, but much closer attention to the accountability of partnerships is essential, as well as the measurement of their impacts and true value to society as a whole. These things cannot be done in simplistic terms. Partnerships are also political processes and many of their achievements will not be directly quantifiable; in particular, their preventive and mitigative successes will be hard to demonstrate. Yet they are the basis for global activity to tackle some of the most serious challenges of the century, and so should not be short-changed on good governance and accountability. This includes the appointment of effective and high-profile leaders and senior management who can develop significant public and political profiles for the partnerships and be directly accountable for their success.

Business as a social actor

As I have argued throughout this book, business is a social actor and therefore will increasingly need social license for its activities. Some have gone further. Paul Polman, the CEO of Unilever, argues that: "We're a non-government organization. The only difference is, we're making money so we are sustainable."[4] This is similar to the way that some of the internet companies might characterize their social role, such as Google's "Don't be Evil" or the establishment of Microsoft's Technology and Human Rights Centre.[5] It is clear that some companies really do feel they have a strong social purpose. In this book, I have made a fundamental distinction between non-state actors whose primary purpose is social and those whose primary purpose is not. The former can claim to be part of the social contract itself, whilst the latter generally are not—their primary responsibility is one of non-infringement, of respecting rights but not protecting or fulfilling them. It is clear that the edges of the envelope are being pushed by both the internet governance debate and the public–private partnership discussion and that the two are, to an extent, interrelated.

If we are to suppose that the primary purpose of business is social, then this might only be sustainable with changes in the governance and market arrangements that set the longer-term priorities for any company. Whilst I am a great admirer of Paul Polman at Unilever, I wonder how much of what he has done will be sustainable when he leaves the company. Is the primary purpose of Unilever still to return a profit to shareholders or do we indeed have a new type of company, one in which social outcomes are valued by the financial markets as much as the financial ones? It might be that we will start to see this shift over the coming years, but until we see fundamental changes in Unilever's own governance arrangements, how can any of us be sure that Unilever will not have reverted to type in ten years' time? I had the privilege of working at The Body Shop when it was a unique company with a publicly stated social mission, but it was, still, at the end of the day, accountable to its shareholders above its stakeholders, and its stakeholders above its rights-holders.

So at the end of the day, it's all about governance, and so too with the internet. We will see over the next ten years whether the digital world really is one where state and non-state actors can work together as equals. If such a change takes place, it will have involved governments giving up some of their usual power and ICT companies becoming much more socially accountable than they are today. The Snowden revelations suggest that governments, or at least their security agencies, do not see the internet as a libertarian exception, but rather—for reasons of national security—that state control is essential. Yet, for the time being, discussions such as those at the annual Stockholm Internet Forum or the Freedom Online Coalition are fascinating multi-stakeholder exchanges on what are some of the fundamental questions of this century. Are we seeing a

"we will see over the next ten years whether the digital world really is one where state and non-state actors can work together as equals"

lasting shift in the nature of the social contract or a more temporary post-Cold War blip that will shortly revert to the leviathan of state control?

What is more certain is that much closer partnerships between governments, business, and civil society will become the new norm and that clearer rules of accountability and governance will be central to their legitimacy. It is therefore likely that each partnership will need social license. We are clearly at a very early stage of such discussions, but let's hope that the 2015 Development Goals from the United Nations will set a clear standard for such partnerships—if not, they will need to be developed elsewhere.

My own belief is that the change is coming, but that it will require more fundamental transformations in how markets and stock exchanges behave before we see a sustainable shift, and before we can really say that businesses are non-state actors that value social outcomes as highly as profit. The test will come when companies are facing financial challenges and are forced to choose between priorities. For civil society organizations, the same dilemma does not exist, or at least should not—their purpose is social or there should be no purpose at all. In the meantime there will be experimentation, and public–private partnerships and multi-stakeholder initiatives will be a key testing ground: how much power are governments and businesses willing to cede to such approaches in exchange for mutually agreed social outcomes? By 2020 there will be more evidence around to show whether such partnerships themselves have become key social actors with their own social license.

chapter 12

The social license—a prognosis

I have tried to make the case throughout the preceding chapters that the broad concept of "social license"—beyond the narrower confines of the more established "social license to operate" that many in business and the CSR community have grown familiar with—is a potentially more meaningful way of thinking about the diverse range of societal relationships that organizations of all kinds must navigate in the 21st century.

I've contended that a holistic understanding of the social license is crucial for effective decision making and responsible action, not only for business, but for organizations of all kinds, including government and those representing civil society. But as I've explained, coming to grips with the full implications of a more expansive notion of the social license will likely pose a different set of questions and challenges for different types of organizations. The fact is that we are still in the very early days of re-imagining a whole range of relationships between public and private, between the state and the market, between consumers and those who produce goods and services that add value to our world.

My aim in this concluding section is not only to bring together the various ideas and concepts I've discussed throughout this book, but also to provide what I hope is a useful starting place for those wishing to engage more deeply on how a social license approach might impact the way we think about our missions and activities in the time ahead. I must warn readers that the guidance I'm offering won't provide a "how to" guide.

In fact, I conclude this book by raising more questions than providing clear answers. This is so both because asking the right questions is key to making further progress and because we haven't arrived at widely agreed pathways forward. So my hope is a modest one—that I might help some readers in beginning to tackle some hard issues and in finding their own constructive ways forward that work for everyone. That for me is what makes the journey so interesting.

The "social license" is defined fully in Chapter 2 of this book, but I would like to remind the reader what some of the key aspects are:

- The social license relates to the activities of any organization and might be defined in relation to an organization's legitimacy in the eyes of society (and the legitimacy of the related activity), the trust stakeholders have in it as well as the consent granted for specific activities by rights-holders. It cannot be directly managed or self-awarded, rather it is the accumulation of a number of factors: Benefits—the delivery of sufficiently positive outcomes for all concerned; tackling imbalances of power—knowledge, participation, transparency, and accountability; and Prevention and remedies—protecting victims and ensuring justice. It is these factors that organizations can manage, not the social license itself.
- It is much easier to notice the absence of the social license than its presence. The presence of the social license might be described as an equitable balance, or harmony, between different interests that allows an activity to continue and to thrive. However, as it is dynamic, it can always be withdrawn.
- The social license relates to what an organization *does* as opposed to what it *is*—i.e. it relates to the activities of an organization.
- The social license should be understood in social contract terms and therefore different types of organization will acquire the social license in different ways for their activities because they have a different relationship to the social contract. The classic distinctions are: for governments, by being accountable and effective servants of the social contract in society; for civil society, it is about strengthening the accountability of government or the strength of the social contract itself, and for business (whose primary purpose is not social) it is about not weakening the social contact or exploiting existing weaknesses—and finding ways of building capacity within the existing social contract without replacing it.

- There is some evidence that on some issues, such as internet governance, dealing with remote communities or international public–private partnerships, business is being granted a much wider social license and is treated as if it were a social actor such as an NGO or even a government.
- The social license does not replace political license or legal license, in fact quite the opposite is the case. However, both legal and political licenses have limitations and they are increasingly reliant on the social license.
- The limitations of existing political and legal license need to be understood in an international context and against international norms such as human rights. Modern interpretations of social contract theory have made much use of human rights and so too does this approach to understanding the social license.

In Chapter 3, I took the example of corporate social responsibility (CSR) to ask if existing approaches for understanding societal relationships were fit for purpose and whether fresh ideas such as the social license might help.

What next for CSR?

Not all that is currently labeled CSR is worthless in fact, a number of important developments and initiatives have sprung from this framework. However, one of the central themes of this book has been that the value of the most effective approaches has been and continues to be, severely diminished by the CSR label. As argued in Chapter Three, CSR has been the only real "show in town" for understanding the interface between business and society. But this does not change the fact that the CSR concept often makes no little sense from the perspective of the social contract—it too often suggests that the social role of business is either a voluntary gesture or is divorced from the primarily non-social purpose of the business itself. The current CSR industry represents an enormous opportunity cost for what really should be the focus of attention.

The emergence of business and human rights as an international movement is also encouraging. The United Nations "Protect, Respect, and Remedy" framework, and the Guiding Principles that flow from it, recognize that government duties, to protect people from abuses caused by or involving non-state actors, including businesses, are central, and that the corporate responsibility to respect rights is also now an international norm. This baseline understanding of "respect," which applies to all business actors, wherever they operate, is achieved through acquiring knowledge, reducing risks, mitigating negative social impacts, being transparent, and providing remedies. This fits well with social contract thinking. I've made the case that the primary purpose of business is not to promote social welfare and therefore it is not a direct part of the social contract that binds society and establishes government; however, it can have a very big impact upon it. As a result, business must ensure, at a minimum, that it does not undermine or weaken this pre-existing contract. The central questions for business, discussed in this book, and the ones that mainstream CSR too often does not address adequately, are:

- Does my business fully respect all human rights, and other international standards, and does it have knowledge of its potential and actual social impacts, risks, and mitigations?
- Is my business sufficiently transparent about these risks, impacts, and mitigations?
- Are rights-holders and stakeholders involved in prioritization and assessing how the business respects human rights?
- Are adequate remedies in place for those rights-holders negatively affected by my business activities? Do these include acknowledging that victims have access to legal remedy and not frustrating due process?

These then are the basic questions that all businesses will need to answer. But we shouldn't underestimate just how much of a challenge this will be. We shouldn't think business needs to do less in social terms than CSR might suggest, quite the inverse; for business to really consider its social impacts would be nothing short of a revolution. True, more businesses ask these questions than five years ago, but most still do not. Nor do governments yet require that businesses do so. However, if we think about the social license, business cannot end there. If the social license requires a business to be in some kind of harmony with the social contract, what happens when the social contract within a specific country is itself weak, undermined, or non-existent? This presents other fundamental questions to any business that need to be addressed.

In situations where it is the government that is overly oppressive, coercive, or corrupt, it is not enough for a business to claim a 'following local law' defence, as the vast majority still will when asked at the height of a crisis, as Yahoo in China in 2008, and Vodafone in Egypt in 2011.[1] The question to be asked by business when entering countries where Hobbes' *Leviathan* is too strong or unaccountable are:

- What additional steps must be taken to ensure that business activities do not lead to further negative impacts on the population in general? This book has posed a number of questions, including:
- What measures can be taken in contractual arrangements with the government to give the business as many safeguards as possible that its services or products will not be used to violate human rights?
- Which rights-holders and stakeholders can participate in the due diligence decision-making and also act as an early warning in terms of heightened risks—not directly to the business itself but to vulnerable rights-holders?
- Does the company have leverage to change any aspects of governmental behavior or to collaborate with the international community to give added protection to the most vulnerable?
- Will the company be able to state any of its concerns publicly?

At the end of the day the company will vote with its feet. It will enter a market and start paying taxes to a government. When it does so, it will be having some impact on the existing social contract. If a company really feels it is better off in a market than out of it—and I would argue that most countries benefit from having a diversity of investment in human rights as well as economic terms—then it needs to demonstrate this. When entering a country where the social contract is dysfunctional, the onus is on a business to show it has not exploited this situation for its own benefit. It is home governments and the international community that must hold businesses accountable to this standard, which is one of healthy skepticism unless the business proves otherwise. There have been some useful examples of such approaches in the USA toward investments in South Africa, Northern Ireland, and Sudan over the past 30 years,[2] where there have been criteria that distinguish between the impacts of specific companies. The USA currently has a specific reporting requirement for US companies investing in Myanmar (Burma). This also should be evaluated over the years ahead to see if it has been effective in social terms. It is notable that European governments are less inclined to take such approaches historically. However, this too might be changing with momentum gathering on issues such as conflict minerals, non-financial reporting, and trafficking/forced labor. Interestingly, when such requirements are linked to bilateral trade agreements, which has been the case with many involving Colombia for example, these requirements can be two-way: the Colombians or Chileans can and will start asking Europeans similar questions.

There are similar concerns when a government is too weak to protect the social contract, as in many poor countries, and business itself may be faced with calls to almost assume the role of government in areas where it has significant activities. Some of the key questions that have emerged here are:

- How does a business help to empower government to perform its duties in relation to human rights and the social contract?
- What are the capacity-related contributions business can make to this endeavor?
- How does the business ensure that it does not become the quasi-government and duty-bearer in the eyes of local populations?

Finally, business needs to understand how it relates to the other party to the social contract: the rights-holders themselves. Very few companies currently focus on rights-holders and prefer to cherry-pick stakeholders (i.e. civil society organizations) according to their own subjective criteria and whether the NGO is "user-friendly." Instead, business should ask:

- How does a business talk directly to the rights-holders who will be the most affected by its activities?
- Which organizations legitimately represent their interests, i.e. which stakeholders should the business involve in dialogue, not because they have the loudest voice, but because they are most material to the social contract?
- How does the business best empower civil society to hold to account both government and powerful organizations like my own?

These are not easy questions but are the questions which emerge when we consider the social license of business in social contract terms. In my opinion, they are the questions that should define the business–society interface for the years to come and are those most closely associated with the social license of business activities. CSR has had the past 20 years to pose such questions and attempt some answers, but it still does not do so in any consistent manner.

Organizations holding each other to account in social contract terms

Every organization needs to know where it sits in terms of the social contract if it is to enjoy social license. The critical questions for rights-holders to ask are:

To a government:

- Does this government serve the interests of its people or just some specific elite or interest group?
- How transparent and accountable is it? (All societies and their governments are corrupt to some extent, as the European Union's (recent and first) Anti-Corruption report recently reminded us, but some are clearly much more corrupt than others[3]).
- As well as ensuring democratic, or some other, legitimate process, how does the government ensure that it has the social license for activities that are high risk or of a controversial nature?
- Given the above, is the government a sufficiently legitimate servant of the social contract between its people?
- Is the government willing to hold non-state actors to account for their violations of human rights, whether they be a business, civil society, a religious group or any other type of organization?

To a civil society organization:

- From what does the legitimacy of the organization derive: from democratic representation of a particular community or interest group, from the internationally recognized norms it espouses, or both? If it is neither, then searching questions should be asked as to whose interests the organization really serves.
- What policies does the organization have in place to strengthen the social contract within society? If the aim of the organization is to weaken the social contract, by creating division, misinformation, hatred, and so on within a particular country, this would suggest that it is not a legitimate organization—unless the government in question is illegitimate in social contract terms. Then the issue is whether the government or the civil society organization is better aligned with international norms, such as human rights. This is one of the most delicate questions of all, if we think of the clampdown against Gay

Rights organizations in Russia in 2013/14 for example. Governments can criminalize the activities of some civil society organizations, but this does not necessarily make such groups criminals within the context of international law—sometimes quite the reverse.

- Does the organization itself align its activities with empowering wider civil society, holding governments to account, or raising the capacity of governments to be better duty-bearers? In other words, does the civil society organization take a rights-based approach, either self-consciously or by default? Civil society organizations that see human rights as irrelevant are, almost by definition, placing themselves outside of the social contract. It is surprising, therefore, how few civil society organizations have really thought about a rights-based approach to their activities (unless they happen to be human rights NGOs, that is).

To a business:

- Does the business consider its social impacts and not just the financial or reputational impacts on the business itself? Is this stated in human rights terms (i.e. is the business "rights-aware")? If not, what is the justification for this? Excuses, such as cultural relativism, avoiding political or religious offense, and ease of communication, are not acceptable in justice-based social contract terms.
- How can the business demonstrate that its activities have at worst a neutral effect on the pre-existing social contract in the societies where it has impacts, and at best a positive effect?
- If there is well founded evidence of negative impact, will the business be willing or able to take adequate remedial or mitigative steps? In the worst case, is the business willing to suspend activities even if there is a short-term economic loss in doing so?
- Whilst it is governments, and their judiciaries, that need to have the ultimate legal leverage over other types of organization, non-state actors can also hold each other to account in social contract terms. All organizations should ask the above questions of each other, whether directly in meetings or through their prior due diligence or both. The lack of adequate answers to the questions above should cause any organization to reflect on whether the organization in question is likely to be a legitimate partner in social license terms.

Some issues to watch over the years ahead

In this book I have given a range of examples from a range of business sectors, countries, and types of civil society organization. It is clear that issues of human rights and the internet will be a focal point for social contract-related discussions over the coming years, in terms of both online content and the governance of the internet itself. At the moment, the internet is controlled by no single actor. It is a "global commons."

However, there are many reasons why this situation might not continue over the coming years, as the commercial interests of a few dominant companies as well as the security and internal control interests of governments start to close in on the libertarian principles that have guided its development to date. In particular, the *right to privacy* will become a common concern, and not just one reserved for politicians and celebrities. The social license online will see a focus of the social contract under which the *Leviathan* of government control will remain contested. At present the interests of non-state actors (business and civil society) are generally aligned in maintaining a social contract in which a range of non-actors, and not just governments, have responsibilities to protect internet freedom. The next decade will see whether this "commons" approach, which owes more to Rousseau's *New Republic* than to Hobbes' *Leviathan*, will persist, and whether it will conform to the rules of national state hegemony that have marked the past 200 years of human history. Social contract thinking can lead to revolutions, as it did during the 18th century in Europe and North America and almost everywhere else in the two centuries that followed. And it is still too early to tell whether the internet will be a mechanism for true social revolution or not. Is the new norm the mobilizing power inherent in ICTs in the early days of the Arab Spring, or instead mass surveillance by governments, as revealed by the Edward Snowden revelations? Sitting here in early 2014, it feels depressingly as if it is the latter—in other words not a new norm at all.

Another issue coming center stage is that of transparency. It is too simplistic to see this as being in opposition to the trend towards privacy previously described. Rather, greater transparency is becoming a societal expectation. Secrets are not generally good for the health of the social contract, and corruption creates perverse incentives for organizations not to act in harmony with it. The types of transparency we now see in oil, gas, and mining revenues in the extractive industries is just the start of it. Organizations will need to be ready to disclose aspects of their activities promptly, partly fueled by mobile technologies that allow secrets to be broken or revealed, whether these be labor abuses in a company's supply chains or the tittle-tattle of embassy communications, as in the case of *Wikileaks*. It is said that the policy makers of the future will not be willing to commit so many of their thoughts and actions to paper and that oral communications are less accountable than written ones. It might be that future biographers will have far fewer written sources to access when trying to get inside the heads of leaders. The transparency debate has yet to settle. In general terms, the increasing expectation of transparency will be good for the social license.

"the increasing expectation of transparency will be good for the social license"

It seems inevitable also that we will expect all of our organizations to be more accountable to us in direct terms. In some ways the social contract is starting to become more diverse and multi-directional. When bad things happen, communities seem increasingly unwilling to let matters rest, even though their advocates might live thousands of miles away all around the world. The hopes of the Arab Spring and the reversals, repression, and communal strife that have followed have not been hidden from the world. Nor have the street protests in countries such as Turkey and Brazil during 2013, or the London riots in 2011. The fact that some powerful businesses have been able to defend their legal and political licenses in defiance of what seems to be natural justice, will be redressed. The outcome of limitations to mechanisms such as the Alien Tort Claims Statute in the United States will build tensions elsewhere in the system, as was the case in 2014 when Latin American and African governments took forward demands for greater corporate accountability to international law. The push towards the greater accountability of non-state actors within the international community has only just started. This is partly political expediency but it is also a reflection of a lack of harmony within what might be seen as an emerging global social contract, where governments seek to act in ways which do not just reflect the concerns (or perceived concerns) of their own people but also play, in part, to wider global audiences.

It is less clear what other forms of mutual accountability will develop along the lines of current multi-stakeholder initiatives—where governments, businesses, and civil society sit together to tackle specific social and environmental challenges. On some issues, such as global health, these partnerships have worked well. In relation to human rights issues, such partnerships have been more fraught and contested, but in many ways cooperation between different types of organization is inevitable. The new set of Development Goals to be issued by the United Nations in 2015 will point heavily to public–private partnerships, and these will need their own social license if they are to be successful.

Where multi-stakeholder initiatives are likely to prosper is where they focus on the other important strand of *accountability*: that of *prevention*. Any organization that neglects health and safety is unlikely to enjoy a social license over the longer term, even in jurisdictions where government enforcement is poor. The same will increasingly become true of other social issues. I have explored in this book due diligence and mitigation cost time and money. They are not absolutes. The central question of how much prevention it is reasonable to expect is a fundamental one and cannot legitimately be answered by an organization on its own. Multi-stakeholder initiatives can be effective processes in agreeing the "threshold of adequacy" in relation to challenges facing specific activities. It is regrettable that nothing similar was in place on deepwater drilling prior to the Gulf of Mexico disaster, and that it still does not exist on that issue in many parts of the world, as well as others such as fracking, tar sands, and nuclear energy. Where are the national public debates on what society expects?

Yes, the public is very bad at understanding risk in an objective way (many of us will routinely speed on the roads and eat bad food, yet then lock every window in our house at night even in low-crime areas). However, politicians need to be a little braver here. They have done it in the fights against corruption, malaria, HIV/AIDS, smoking, and even increasingly in the fights against diabetes and obesity, so why not on other issues? In the years to come we might see more national and international commissions set up to provide such impartial multi-stakeholder spaces providing a range of perspectives to complex problems. For tabloid newspapers around the world this will be an easy target, but wisdom has never sold many newspapers or won elections for populist candidates. Some ombudsmen, special rapporteurs, national human rights institutions, and other bodies play this role at present, but they are few and far between, and the truly effective examples are even fewer. They will come: the "prevention question" can be answered in no other way. Even when the due diligence requirement is legislated at the national or international level (as often it needs to be), it is only enforceable if the requirements are seen as legitimate by different organizations.

End note—back to Macondo

This book ends where it started, in Macondo—this time, however, in the original "Macondo." Perhaps, in hindsight, BP was tempting fate when it chose the name. Macondo was a fictional town in Colombia created by Gabriel García Márquez. In the novel *One Hundred Years of Solitude,* when the banana company arrived in Macondo, it brought with it modernity as well as its consequences.[4] With a typical flourish of magical realism, García Márquez wrote that the company "changed the pattern of the rains, accelerated the cycle of harvests and moved the river from where it had always been." But it also unleashed a "wave of bullets" on striking workers in the plaza. Although the town of Macondo was fictional, he was inspired by a real incident on 6 December 1928 in the town of Cienaga in Santa Marta. The workers at the plantation of the United Fruit Company wanted written contracts, eight-hour workdays, and six-day workweeks, and when they could not get these, they went on a strike that went on for more than a month. The government of the United States threatened to send troops unless the company's interests were protected. Colombia sent troops to ward off an American incursion; and an unknown number of workers died in the incidents that followed.

If the social license means anything, it means that events such as those in Cienaga in 1928 should reside in the realms of fiction rather than in reality by the time we reach 2028. To get there the social license needs to be well defined, perhaps in some of the ways set out in this book. All organizations need to ask themselves tough questions about the real nature of their social purpose and whether they are really acquiring the necessary knowledge about their activities to build social license. Tougher questions need to be asked of businesses when they make sweeping CSR claims, but so too of NGOs and governments when they claim to be acting in the public interest. If societies are to make the right decisions about some of the big decisions on future energy policy, climate change, infrastructure, security, and economic development, then I believe organizations will also have to navigate the social license of their activities, whether through choice or by necessity.

Notes

Chapter 1: Macondo

1. John Locke quoted in *Two Treaties of Government*, comments in edited version by P. Laslett, Cambridge, Cambridge University Press, 1988.
2. National Commission on the BP Deepwater Horizon Oil Spill and Offshore Drilling, *Macondo: The Gulf Oil Disaster, Chief Counsel's Report*, 2011.
3. Frontline, *The Spill*, Public Broadcast Television, USA, 2010.
4. http://www.nytimes.com/2010/06/16/business/16oil.html?_r=0.
5. http://www.bp.com/en/global/corporate/gulf-of-mexico-restoration/deepwater-horizon-accident-and-response/compensating-the-people-and-communities-affected.html.
6. Tom Bergin, *Spills and Spin: The Inside Story of BP*, London, Random House, 2010. *Financial Times*, 5 July 2013.
7. *The United Nations Guiding Principles on Business and Human Rights* agreed by all member States of the UN Human Rights Council in June 2011.
8. Daniel Franks et al. (2014) "Conflict translates environmental and social risks into business costs," Proceedings of the National Academy of Sciences, Australia.
9. Neil Gunningham, Robert Kagan, and Dorothy Thornton (2004) "Social License and Environmental Protection: Why Businesses Go beyond Compliance," Berkeley Law Scholarship Repository, 1 January 2004.
10. Lecture given by Tony Hayward to the Stanford Business School in July 2009.
11. See, for example, Bergin, *Spills and Spin*.
12. For a good personal overview of BP's achievements see Christine Bader, *The Evolution of a Corporate Idealist*, Bibliomotion, MA, USA, 2014.
13. http://www.voluntaryprinciples.org.
14. The Extractive Industries Transparency Initiative, http://www.eiti.org.
15. The Voluntary Principles on Security and Human Rights, http://www.voluntaryprinciples.org.

16. http://www.theguardian.com/world/2014/feb/24/bangladesh-factory-collapse-big-brands-urged-pay-help-fund.
17. *Financial Times*, 5 July 2013.
18. *Mohandas Karamchand Gandhi* (1960), compiled by Ravindra Kelekar, Trusteeship, April 1960, printed and published by Jitendra T. Desai Navajivan Mudranalaya.

Chapter 2: The social license

1. Excerpt from the final statement made (but not allowed to be read in court) by Ken Saro-Wiwa before he was executed on 10 November 1995 along with eight other leaders of the Ogoni people, http://www.colorado.edu/journals/standards/V5N2/ESSAYS/wiwa.html.
2. United Nations Environment Programme, *Environmental Assessment of Ogoniland*, Nairobi, Kenya, UNEP, 2011.
3. UNEP, *Environmental Assessment*.
4. James Wilsdon and Rebecca Willis (2004) *See-through Science: Why public engagement needs to move upstream*, Demos, UK.
5. Mureau (2000) cited in Jacqueline Williams and Paul Martin (eds.) *Defining the Social License of Farming: Directions in Agriculture*, Collingwood, Australia, CSIRO Publishing, 2011.
6. Cited in Leeora Black, *The Social License to Operate: Your Management Framework for Complex Times*, Oxford, Do Sustainability, 2013.
7. Robert Boutilier and Ian Thomson, *Modelling and Measuring, The Social License to Operate: Fruits of a Dialogue between Theory and Practice*, 2012, http://socialicense.com.
8. Leeora Black, *The Very Seductive Social License to Operate – a Reality Check*, 2012, http://www.probonoaustralia.com.au/news/2012/10/very-seductive-social-license-operate-%E2%80%93-reality-check#sthash.7Ix2jCV3.dpuf.
9. Leeora Black, *The Social License to Operate*.
10. Interview with Bruce Harvey, Global Practice Leader, Communities and Social Performance, Rio Tinto, *Achieve*, Sinclair Knight Merz, 2011.
11. OECD, *Foreign Direct Investment and the Environment: Lessons from the Mining Sector*, OECD Global Forum on International Investment, Paris, OECD, 2002.
12. See, for example, John Ruggie, "Consultation on operationalizing the framework for business and human rights presented by the Special Representative of the Secretary-General on the issue of human rights and transnational corporations and other business enterprises," Keynote speech, Palais des Nations, Geneva, 5–6 October 2009.

13. James Anaya, "Extractive industries that operate within or near indigenous territories,", Geneva, United Nations, Report A/HRC/18/35, 2011.

14. Jacqueline Williams and Paul Martin (eds.), *Defining the Social License of Farming: Directions in Agriculture*, Collingwood, Australia, CSIRO Publishing, 2011.

15. Oxfam, *Community Consent Index*, Boston, Oxfam America, 2012.

16. Luke Malpass, "Rule of Law or Social License to Operate?," *New Zealand Business Review*, 16 August 2013. http://nzinitiative.org.nz/Media/Opinion+and+commentary/Rule+of+law+or+social+license+to+operate.html.

17. Malpass, "Rule of law or social license to operate?"

18. For example, Justine Lacey and Julian Lamont "Using Social Contract to Inform Social Licence to Operate: An Application in the Australian Coal Seam Gas Industry," *Journal of Cleaner Production*, 30 (2013), 1–9.

19. Thomas Hobbes, *Leviathan or The Matter, Forme and Power of a Common Wealth Ecclesiasticall and Civil*, London, 1651.

20. John Locke, *Second Treatise of Government*, London, 1689.

21. Jean-Jacques Rousseau, *Du contrat social*, Paris, 1762.

22. Lother Auchter and Martin Dziewa, "Managing Business Values in a Globalized Economy by Integrated Social Contract Theory," *The Business and Management Review*, vol. 3(2), January 2013.

23. Dorota Pietrzyk, "Civil Society – a conceptual history from Hobbes to Marx," *Marie Curie Working Papers No. 1*, Department of International Politics, University of Wales, 2001.

24. http://www.marcgunther.com/paul-polman-a-radical-ceo/?utm_source=feedburner&utm_medium=email&utm_campaign=Feed%3A+MarcGunther+%28Marc+Gunther%29.

25. Guizot, "Philosophie politique" quoted in Jeremy Jennings, "Rousseau, social contract and the modern Leviathan," in *The Social Contract from Hobbes to Rawls*, ed. David Boucher and Paul Kelly, London, Routledge, 1994.

Chapter 3: What's wrong with CSR?

1. Geoffrey Chandler "The Curse of Corporate Social Responsibility," in John Morrison (ed.) *New Academy Review*, 2(1), Spring 2003, University of Cambridge Programme for Industry/KPMG.

2. But to be fair to the often-misquoted Milton Friedman, even he gave business carte blanche: "There is only one and only one social responsibility of business—to use its resources and engage in activities designed to increase its profits so long as it stays within the rules of the game, which is to say, engages in open and free competition without deception or fraud."

3. http://www.unido.org/en/what-we-do/trade/csr/what-is-csr.html.
4. http://ec.europa.eu/enterprise/policies/sustainable-business/corporate-social-responsibility/index_en.htm.
5. http://www.oecd.org/corporate/mne/corporateresponsibilityfrequentlyasked questions.htm.
6. http://www.iso.org/iso/home/standards/iso26000.htm.
7. Michael Porter and Mark Kramer, "Creating Shared Value," *Harvard Business Review*, 89(1/2) Jan/Feb 2011, pp. 62–77.

Chapter 4: Legitimacy

1. Jean-Jacques Rousseau (1762).
2. Loomis, "Legitimacy Norms as Change Agents: Examining the Role of the Public Voice," in *Legality and Legitimacy in Global Affairs*, ed. Richard Falk, Mark Juergensmeyer and Vesselin Popovski, Oxford Scholarship Online 2012.
3. See Carolin Decker, *Legitimacy Needs as Drivers of Business Exit*, Gabler, Wiesbaden, 2007.
4. Porter, "How Big Business Can Regain Legitimacy," commentary for *Bloomberg Businessweek*, 6 May 2010.
5. Green, "Competitive Theory and Business Legitimacy," commentary for *Bloomberg Businessweek*, 22 June 2010.
6. A good book on the history of human rights organizations and their related legitimacy is that by Aryeh Neier, *The International Human Rights Movement: A History*, Princeton University Press, Princeton, 2012.
7. http://news.bbc.co.uk/2/hi/south_asia/8725140.stm.
8. http://money.msn.com/top-stocks/post.aspx?post=69bccaa7-7ec9-41a5-815c-4fbb8062c426.
9. Broughton, "The Bhopal Disaster and its Aftermath: A Review," *Environmental Health*, 4(6), May 2005.
10. http://www.businessweek.com/stories/2008-05-27/dow-chemical-liable-for-bhopal.
11. ww.sakaaltimes.com/NewsDetails.aspx?NewsId=4904706774648512323&SectionId=5171561142064258099&SectionName=Pune&NewsDate=20100909&NewsTitle=Dow%20decides%20to%20quit%20Chakan.
12. http://www.businessweek.com/stories/2008-05-27/dow-chemical-liable-for-bhopal.
13. Julian Assange, "Thought for the Day," *Today Programme*, BBC Radio 4, 2 January 2014.
14. Snowden himself did not select what was to be published and therefore the disclosures were not targeted by him. Snowden "scraped" thousands of

documents from NSA servers and passed them to journalists he respected, wanting them to exercise editorial judgement. It was then up to the *Washington Post*, the *Guardian* and *Der Spiegel* to decide what was published and what should be redacted from the publications. This was supposed to be the case with *Wikileaks*. Assange was in partnership with the *Guardian* but the *Guardian* wanted to go through everything and redact certain names. Assange disagreed and eventually went ahead and dumped the whole cache from Bradley Manning on the Wikileaks website, unredacted.

Chapter 5: Trust

1. Abraham Lincoln (1854) Speech at Clinton, Illinois, 8 September 1854.
2. For example, Robert Boutilier and Ian Thomson, *Modelling and Measuring, The Social License to Operate: Fruits of a Dialogue between Theory and Practice*, 2012, http://socialicense.com., or Leeora Black, *The Social License to Operate: Your Management Framework for Complex Times*, Oxford, Do Sustainability, 2013.
3. Russell Hardin, "Government without Trust," *Journal of Trust Research*, 3(1), 2013.
4. http://trust.edelman.com.
5. Edelman 2012 Trust Barometer, London.
6. http://www.rdtrustedbrands.com/tables/community.shtml.
7. Africa Progress Panel, *Equity in Extractives*, Africa Progress Report, 2013. http://www.africaprogresspanel.org/publications/policy-papers/africa-progress-report-2013/.
8. Guido Möllering, "Trust without knowledge? Comment on Hardin, 'Government without trust'," *Journal of Trust Research*, 3(1), 2013.
9. www.globescan.com.
10. http://www.globescan.com/component/edocman/?view=document&id=87&Itemid=591.
11. http://www.globescan.com/reputation-and-issues-tracking?show=pharmaceutical.
12. GlobeScan, *The IT Industry: Issues and Reputation*, A GlobeScan Stakeholder Intelligence eBrief, 5 September 2013.
13. "The Resource Curse" is shorthand for the observation that many of the African and Asian countries blessed with considerable natural resources have also be beset by civil wars, corruption, and pollution, due in part to the mismanagement of said resources. A number of intergovernmental initiatives have been put in place to try to break this curse, such as the Kimberley Process dealing with so-called "blood diamonds" and the Extractive Industries Transparency Initiative (EITI) relating to mining, oil, and gas more generally.
14. $30 trillion as of April 2013. http://www.unpri.org.

Chapter 6: Consent

1 Personal communication with author following a meeting in Bogotá, Colombia.
2. Recounted to me during an interview with a mining company representative.
3. United Nations, Report on the Special Rapporteur on the Rights of Indigenous Peoples, A/66/288, United Nations General Assembly, New York, 10 August 2011.
4. http://undesadspd.org/IndigenousPeoples/DeclarationontheRightsofIndigenousPeoples.aspx.
5. United Nations, Expert Mechanism Advice No. 2 relating to Indigenous peoples and the right to participate in decision-making, Office of the High Commissioner for Human Rights, Geneva, 2011.
6. "Where the relocation of these peoples is considered necessary as an exceptional measure, such relocation shall take place only with their free and informed consent. Where their consent cannot be obtained, such relocation shall take place only following appropriate procedures established by national laws and regulations, including public inquiries where appropriate, which provide the opportunity for effective representation of the peoples concerned." ILO Convention 169, Indigenous and Tribal Peoples Convention, entered into force on 5 September 1991, Article 16.
7. http://firstpeoples.org/wp/mining-councils-new-commitment-to-fpic-falls-short/.
8. Case of the Saramaka People v. Suriname, Judgment, IACHR, Series C, No. 172 (28 November 2007).
9. International Council on Mining and Metals, Indigenous Peoples and Mining, Position Statement, London, May 2013.
10. Amy Lehr, "Indigenous Peoples' Rights and the Role of Free, Prior and Informed Consent," Good Practice Note, UN Global Compact, 20 February 2014.
11. Lehr, "Indigenous Peoples' Rights."
12. Oxfam, Guide to Free, Prior and Informed Consent, Oxfam Australia, Victoria, 2010.
13. Oxfam, Community Consent Index, Boston, Oxfam America, 2012.
14. Excerpt from the Declaration of Independence of the United States (1776), second paragraph.
15. Universal Declaration of Human Rights (1948), Article 21.
16. Sherry Arnstein, "A Ladder of Citizen Participation," Journal of the American Institute of Planners, 13(4), 1969.
17. Doran Hanlon analyzes the consultation relating to fracking in the UK against Sherry Arnstein's "ladder of citizen participation," University of Sussex, Political Science dissertation, 2014.
18. http://www.itu.int/net/pressoffice/press_releases/2012/39.aspx#.UsiCMRagQts.

19. Rebecca MacKinnon, Consent of the Networked: The Worldwide Struggle for Internet Freedom, New York, Basic Books, 2012.
20. MacKinnon, Consent of the Networked.

Chapter 7: Benefits

1. Salil Tripathi is a journalist and well-known thinker on business and human rights issues. I am also proud to call him a friend and so the quote (which he has given many times) has been repeated numerous times over the last 15 years.
2. http://www.jainworld.com/education/stories25.asp.
3. Wentang Tang and William Parish, *Chinese Urban Life under Reform: The Changing Social Context*, Cambridge, Cambridge University Press, 2000.
4. Tang and Parish, *Chinese Urban Life*.
5. European Commission, *Europe 2020 in a nutshell*, http://ec.europa.eu/europe2020/europe-2020-in-a-nutshell/index_en.htm.
6. United Nations, *Universal Declaration of Human Rights*, Palais de Chaillot, Paris, 10 December 1948.
7. Stephen Angle (2008) "Human Rights and Harmony", *Human Rights Quarterly*, 30: 76–94.
8. http://www.unilever.com/sustainable-living/betterlivelihoods/impact-studies/indonesia/.
9. Oxfam, *Labour rights in Unilever's Supply Chain: From Compliance towards Good Practice*, January 2013.
10. http://politicsofpoverty.oxfamamerica.org/2011/03/oxfam-america-explores-coca-cola-sabmiller-value-chain-impact-on-poverty-reduction.

Chapter 8: Tackling imbalances of power

1. Thomas Paine. *Rights of Man*, London, J.S. Jordan, 1791. Following its publication, Paine never again returned to England due to the charge of seditious libel against the British Crown.
2. Aung San Suu Kyi, *Freedom from Fear*, London, Penguin Books, 1991.
3. BLIHR (Business Leaders Initiative on Human Rights), "Newmont: Taking a rights-aware approach to the development of the Ahafo Mine in Ghana,"," The Millennium Development Goals and Human Rights, with the Institute for Human Rights and Business and the Corporate Social Responsibility Initiative, Harvard Kennedy School, 2009.
4. BLIHR, "Newmont."

5. BLIHR, "Newmont."
6. http://www.oneworldtrust.org/globalaccountability/gar.
7. Parliamentary Commission on Banking Standards, *Changing Banking for Good*, 12 June 2013, quoted in http://blogs.reuters.com/financial-regulatory-forum/2013/09/11/reforming-bankings-risk-culture-requires-breaking-accountability-firewall/.
8. http://www.theguardian.com/business/2013/oct/23/gsk-china-corruption-scandal-glaxosmithkline.

Chapter 9: Prevention and remedies

1. Edmund Burke (1783) Speech relating to the East India Bill, 1 December 1783, British Parliament, London.
2. Institute for Human Rights and Business, *Human Rights within the Political Economy of States: avenues for application*, London, IHRB, 2014.
3. See FAFO, Business and International Crimes, www.fafo.no/liabilities.
4. UN SRSG, A/HRC/8/5 "Protect, Respect and Remedy: a Framework for Business and Human Rights", 7 April 2008, p. 23. http://www.reports-and-materials.org/Ruggie-report-7-Apr-2008.pdf.
5. Commentary to Guiding Principle 26.
6. See the civil society statement in support of the statement made to the Human Rights Council by Ecuador on behalf of the Africa Group, the Arab Group, Pakistan, Sri Lanka, Kyrgyzstan, Cuba, Nicaragua, Bolivia, Venezuela, and Peru. http://www.tni.org/sites/www.tni.org/files/statement_in_support_of_states_at_the_hrc_enesp_17092013.pdf and http://cancilleria.gob.ec/wp-content/uploads/2013/09/DECLARACION.pdf (in Spanish only).
7. See FAFO, Business and International Crimes, www.fafo.no/liabilities. Regarding European countries, see also Clifford Chance, "Corporate Liability in Europe", 2012. http://www.cliffordchance.com/content/dam/cliffordchance/PDF/European_Technical_Bulletin.pdf.
8. See also a recent update to ICAR's due diligence report: Mark Taylor, "Human Rights Due Diligence: The Role of States – 2013 Progress Report".
9. Such as the Dutch public prosecutors clarification that it considers business activity in the Israeli-occupied West Bank, noting such activities could be a potential war crime and suggesting Dutch companies take concrete steps to end their activities in the area. See also, Taylor, "Human Rights Due Diligence", p.11.http://accountabilityroundtable.org/analysis/human-rights-due-diligence-2013-update/.
10. Recently for example, a Swiss probe into a gold refiner accused in a criminal complaint by a Swiss NGO of suspected money laundering in connection

with alleged war crimes in the DRC, see: http://www.reuters.com/article/ 2013/11/04/congo-gold-idUSL5N0IP29K20131104#comments; a French judicial investigation into the sale of a surveillance system to the Gaddafi regime in Libya filed by FIDH and LDH, see also: http://www.refworld.org/docid/ 511cb668a.html; and a German complaint about a timber manufacturer's senior manager regarding abuses by its contracted security forces against a community in the DRC, see also: http://www.ecchr.de/index.php/danzer-en. html.

11. Taylor, "Human Rights Due Diligence", p. 5. http://accountabilityroundtable. org/analysis/human-rights-due-diligence-2013-update/.

12. Ibid.

13. For further background on the case, see: http://business-humanrights.org/ media/documents/kiobel-supreme-court-17apr-2013.pdf.

14. See, for example, ICAR and EarthRights International's "Nation-wide law school partnership project", where Loyola University, New Orleans College of Law, New England Law (Boston), Santa Clara Law, UCLA School of Law, University of Oregon School of Law, University of Virginia School of Law, Western New England University School of Law, and Rutgers School of Law–Camden will research state law and propose recommendations and draft legislation for legal reform around corporate accountability in their state.

15. As reported in ICAR, "Human Rights Due Diligence: The Role of States – 2013 Progress Report", p. 6. http://accountabilityroundtable.org/analysis/ human-rights-due-diligence-2013-update/.

16. Ibid.

17. In France for example, Act No. 2008-757 imposes administrative liability on companies to encourage them to conduct environmental due diligence, with clear human rights implications involved in many potential scenarios the liability is covering. It states: "In cases of imminent threat of injury, the operator shall, without delay and at his expense, take preventative measures in order to prevent the occurrence or mitigate its effects. If the threat persists, it shall promptly inform the authority … of its nature, of the prevention measures it has taken and of their results." See further ICAR, "Human Rights Due Diligence: The Role of States", p. 20.http://accountabilityroundtable.org/wp-content/ uploads/2012/12/Human-Rights-Due-Diligence-The-Role-of-States.pdf.

18. http://www.ccohs.ca/oshanswers/legisl/diligence.html.

19. http://english.mofcom.gov.cn/aarticle/newsrelease/press/201203/ 20120308015346.htm and http://www.gov.cn/gzdt/2010-08/18/content_1682 340.htm.

20. http://wetten.overheid.nl/BWBR0007149/geldigheidsdatum_08-10-2012.

21. See ICAR, "Human Rights Due Diligence: The Role of States", pp. 22–4. http://accountabilityroundtable.org/wp-content/uploads/2012/12/Human-Rights-Due-Diligence-The-Role-of-States.pdf.

22. As noted in ICAR, "Human Rights Due Diligence: The Role of States", see also: US Sentencing Guidelines Manual, para. 8D1.4, p. 527. http://www.ussc.gov/Guidelines/2012_Guidelines/Manual_PDF/Chapter_8.pdf.
23. For a comprehensive discussion of extraterritoriality in a range of regulatory contexts, see: Jennifer Zerk, "Extraterritorial Jurisdiction: Lessons for the Business and Human Rights Sphere from Six Regulatory Areas", Harvard Corporate Social Responsibility Initiative, 2010, 163–9. http://www.hks.harvard.edu/m-rcbg/CSRI/publications/workingpaper_59_zerk.pdf.
24. For example, the US Presidential Administration of George Bush took a different philosophical and political stance on the question of corporate liability under the US Alien Tort Claims Act than the subsequent Obama Administration. Moreover, the US Government opinion during the Obama Administration changed during the course of a single case under the Act. The case also elicited a range of views from the German, Dutch, and UK Governments, as well as from the European Commission. See also: http://www.scotusblog.com/case-files/cases/kiobel-v-royal-dutch-petroleum/.
25. The United Nations Guiding Principles on Business and Human Rights agreed by all member States of the UN Human Rights Council in June 2011.
26. Zerk, "Extraterritorial Jurisdiction", p. 23. http://www.hks.harvard.edu/m-rcbg/CSRI/publications/workingpaper_59_zerk.pdf.
27. See the case of Chandler v Cape plc (25 April 2012), at: http://www.business-humanrights.org/Links/Repository/1012578/jump. See also: http://www.business-humanrights.org/Links/Repository/1012519/jump.
28. As will be explored by the Inter-American Commission on Human Rights, which recently announced that it will consider "home country liability" for the extraterritorial actions of their companies abroad. See: http://www.earthrights.org/blog/inter-american-commission-human-rights-consider-home-country-liability-extraterritorial-actions.
29. See, for example, Institute for Human Rights and Business and the UK Government "Update on the role of OECD National Contact Points with regard to the extractive sectors", London, 22 March 2013; or Institute for Human Rights and Business and the Norwegian NCP, "Multinational Enterprises, Human Rights and Internet Freedom", 27 June 2013, OECD Conference Centre, Paris.

Chapter 10: Different organizations and the social license

1. Lucius Annaeus Seneca (54) Apocolocyntosis, 9:9.
2. https://www.chinadialogue.net/article/show/single/en/4852-Chinese-power-Burmese-politics.

3. http://www.telecoms.com/218501/deutsche-telekom-nsagchq-revelations-an-opportunity/.
4. http://www.telecoms.com/218501/deutsche-telekom-nsagchq-revelations-an-opportunity/.
5. http://www.bbc.co.uk/science/0/21970879.
6. http://news.bbc.co.uk/onthisday/hi/dates/stories/july/10/newsid_2499000/2499283.stm.
7. http://www.bbc.com/news/uk-23097444.
8. John F. Kennedy, Inaugural address as President of the United States of America, 20 January 1961, Washington DC.

Chapter 11: A basis for partnership and accountability

1. Eleanor Roosevelt, "In Our Hands" (1958 speech delivered on the tenth anniversary of the Universal Declaration of Human Rights).
2. See http://www.brookings.edu/blogs/up-front/posts/2014/05/27-mobilizing-private-investment-kharas-mcarthur.
3. Such as the MSI Integrity project, http://www.msi-integrity.org.
4. http://www.marcgunther.com/paul-polman-a-radical-ceo/?utm_source=feedburner&utm_medium=email&utm_campaign=Feed%3A+MarcGunther+%28Marc+Gunther%29.
5. http://www.microsoft.com/about/corporatecitizenship/en-us/working-responsibly/principled-business-practices/HumanRightsCenter.aspx.

Chapter 12: The social license—a prognosis

1. http://www.ihrb.org/commentary/staff/internet_providers_in_egypt.html.
2. The Sullivan Principles in relation to South Africa, the MacBride Principles in relation to Northern Ireland and the Sudan Divestment Task Force.
3. European Commission (2014) Anti-corruption report, DG Home Affairs, Brussels, http://ec.europa.eu/dgs/home-affairs/what-we-do/policies/organized-crime-and-human-trafficking/corruption/anti-corruption-report/index_en.htm.
4. Gabriel García Márquez, *One Hundred Years of Solitude*, London, Jonathan Cape, 1970.

Select Bibliography

Anaya, James, "Extractive industries that operate within or near indigenous territories," United Nations, *Report A/HRC/18/35*, Geneva, 2011.

Andreopoulos, George, Zehra Fabasakal Arat, and Peter Juviler (eds.), *Non-State Actors in the Human Rights Universe*, Bloomfield CT, Kumarian, 2006.

Stephen Angle, "Human rights and harmony," *Human Rights Quarterly* 30 (2008), 76–94.

Sherry Arnstein, "A ladder of citizen participation," *Journal of the American Institute of Planners* 13/4 (1969).

Auchter, Lother and Martin Dziewa, "Managing business values in a globalized economy by integrated social contract theory," *The Business and Management Review*, 3/2 (2013).

Bader, Christine, *The Evolution of a Corporate Idealist*, Bibliomotion, MA, 2014.

Black, Leeora, *The Very Seductive Social Licence to Operate: A Reality Check*, Probono Australia, 31 October 2012.

Black, Leeora, *The Social Licence to Operate: Your Management Framework for Complex Times*, Do Sustainability, Oxford, 2013.

Bergin, Tom, *Spills and Spin: The Inside Story of BP*, London, Random House, 2010.

Boutilier, Robert and Ian Thomson, *Modelling and Measuring, The Social Licence to Operate: Fruits of a Dialogue between Theory and Practice*, 2012.

Business Leaders Initiative on Human Rights, *The Millennium Development Goals and Human Rights*, with the Institute for Human Rights and Business and the Corporate Social Responsibility Initiative, Harvard Kennedy School, 2009.

Chandler, Geoffrey, "The curse of corporate social responsibility," in John Morrison (ed.), *New Academy Review* 2/1 (2003), University of Cambridge Programme for Industry/KPMG.

Franks, Daniel et al, "Conflict translates environmental and social risks into business costs," Proceedings of the National Academy of Sciences, Australia, 2014.

Gunningham, Neil, Robert Kagan, and Dorothy Thornton, 'Social License and Environmental Protection: Why Businesses go beyond compliance', Berkeley Law Scholarship Repository, 1 January 2004.

Hardin, Russell, "Government without trust," *Journal of Trust Research* 3/1 (2013).

Hobbes, Thomas, *Leviathan or The Matter, Forme and Power of a Common Wealth Ecclesiasticall and Civil*, London, 1651.

IHRB (Institute for Human Rights) and Business and the Global Business Initiative on Human Rights, *State of Play Two: The Corporate Responsibility to Respect Human Rights in Business Relationships*, London, IHRB, 2012.

IHRB (Institute for Human Rights) and Business and the UK Government, *Update on the role of OECD National Contact Points with regard to the extractive sectors*, London, 22 March 2013.

IHRB (Institute for Human Rights) and Business and the Norwegian National Contact Point, *Multinational Enterprises, Human Rights and Internet Freedom*, Paris, OECD Conference Centre, 27 June 2013.

Institute for Human Rights and Business, *State of Play Three: Human Rights within the Political Economy of States: Avenues for application*, London, IHRB, 2014.

Karnini, Aneel, "Mandatory CSR in India: A Bad Proposal," *Stanford Social Innovation Review*, Stanford University, CA, 20 May 2013.

Kelekar, Ravindra, *Mohandas Karamchand Gandhi*, Trusteeship, April 1960, Printed and published by Jitendra T. Desai Navajivan Mudranalaya, 1960.

Lacey, Justine, and Julian Lamont, "Using social contract to inform social licence to operate: an application in the Australian coal seam gas industry," *Journal of Cleaner Production* 30 (2013), 1–9.

Lehr, Amy, "Indigenous Peoples' Rights and the Role of Free, Prior and Informed Consent," *Good Practice Note*, UN Global Compact, 20 February 2014.

Lincoln, Abraham, Speech at Clinton, Illinois, 8 September 1854.

Locke, John, *Second Treatise of Government*, London, 1689.

MacKinnon, Rebecca, *Consent of the Networked: The Worldwide Struggle for Internet Freedom*, Basic Books, New York, 2012.

Malpass, Luke, "Rule of law or social licence to operate?" *New Zealand Business Review*, 16 August 2013.

Márquez, Gabriel García, *One Hundred Years of Solitude*, London, Jonathan Cape, 1970.

Neier, Aryeh, *The International Human Rights Movement: A History*, Princeton, Princeton University Press, 2012.

Oxfam, *Guide to Free, Prior and Informed Consent*, Victoria, Oxfam Australia, 2010.

Oxfam, *Community Consent Index*, Boston, Oxfam America, 2012.

Oxfam, *Labour rights in Unilever's Supply Chain: From Compliance towards Good Practice*, January 2013.

Paine, Thomas, *Rights of Man*, London, J.S. Jordan, 1791.

Piketty, Thomas, *Capital in the Twenty-First Century*, Cambridge, MA, Harvard University Press, 2014.

Porter, Michael, *The Competitive Advantage of Nations*, Basingstoke and New York, Palgrave Macmillan, 1990.

Porter, Michael and Mark Kramer, "Creating shared value," *Harvard Business Review* 89/1–2 (2011), 62–77.

Robinson, Mary, *Everybody Matters: A Memoir*, London, Hodder and Stroughton, 2012.

Roddick, Anita, *Business as Unusual*, London, Thorsons, 2000.

Rousseau, Jean-Jacques, *Du contrat social*, Paris, 1762.

Ruggie, John, "Consultation on operationalizing the framework for business and human rights presented by the Special Representative of the Secretary-General on the issue of human rights and transnational corporations and other business enterprises," *Keynote speech*, Geneva, Palais des Nations, 5–6 October 2009.

Ruggie, John, *Just Business: Multinational Corporations and Human Rights*, London, W.W. Norton, 2013.

Sen, Amartya, *Development as Freedom*, New York, Anchor Books, 1999.

Sen, Amartya, *The Idea of Justice*, London, Allen Lane, 2009.

Suu Kyi, Aung San, *Freedom from Fear*, London, Penguin Books, 1991.

Taylor, Mark, *Human Rights Due Diligence: The Role of States – 2013 Progress Report*, Washington DC, International Corporate Accountability Roundtable, 2013.

Williams, Jacqueline and Paul Martin (eds.), *Defining the Social Licence of Farming: Directions in Agriculture*, Collingwood, Australia, CSIRO Publishing, 2011.

Wilsdon, James and Rebecca Willis, *See-through Science: Why public engagement needs to move upstream*, Demos, UK, 2004.

Zerk, Jennifer, "Extraterritorial jurisdiction: Lessons for the business and human rights sphere from six regulatory areas", Harvard Corporate Social Responsibility Initiative, 2010, 163–9.

Index

Printed and bound by CPI Group (UK) Ltd, Croydon, CR0 4YY